HG
2491
.N3
1979

COMMERCIAL
BANKING
in the
ECONOMY

D1202812

JACKSON LIBRARY
LANDER COLLEGE
GREENWOOD, S. C. 29649

OCLC

DCLC

Commercial Banking in the Economy

THIRD EDITION

677859

Paul S. Nadler
Rutgers University

 RANDOM HOUSE • New York

JACKSON LIBRARY
LANDER
GREENWOOD,

OCLC

Third Edition

987654321

Copyright © 1968, 1973, 1979 by Random House, Inc.

All rights reserved under International and Pan-American Copyright Conventions. No part of this book may be reproduced in any form or by any means, electronic or mechanical, including photocopying, without permission in writing from the publisher. All inquiries should be addressed to Random House, Inc., 201 East 50th Street, New York, N.Y. 10022. Published in the United States by Random House, Inc., and simultaneously in Canada by Random House of Canada Limited, Toronto.

Library of Congress Cataloging in Publication Data

Nadler, Paul S.
    Commercial banking in the economy.

    Bibliography: p.
    Includes index.
    1. Banks and banking—United States. I. Title.
HG2491/N3 1979   332.1'2'0973   78-16301
ISBN 0-394-32271-1

MANUFACTURED IN THE UNITED STATES OF AMERICA

Acknowledgment is hereby made for permission to quote from the following works.

Table 1—with permission of Salomon Brothers, New York.

Portions of Chapter Ten—abstracted from an article by the author in *The Bankers Magazine,* January–February, 1978 (New York: Warren, Gorham & Lamont, Inc., 1978), with permission of the publisher.

Portions of Chapter Twelve—abstracted from an article by the author in *The Bankers Handbook,* edited by William H. Baughn and Charles E. Walker (Homewood, Ill.: Dow Jones-Irwin, 1978), with permission of the publisher.

Typography by Lorraine Hohman

Cover design by Jim McKeen

For Julie

Preface to the Third Edition

In the decade since this volume first appeared, banking practices have changed dramatically. Leaders of the industry have experimented with buying their way out of credit restraint through aggressive liability management, only to see serious repercussions in the 1973–1974 credit crunch. Similarly the efforts to expand beyond banking into a number of related services have also been reversed, as bankers learned the adverse side of aggressive diversification efforts.

Many a young banker who had thought that the industry was loaded with old conservatives who needed to learn about "new banking" have by now come to the conclusion that their elders knew a great deal and that banking has risks that remain undiminished no matter how our economy changes.

Moreover bankers have seen competition come from new areas —notably diversification efforts of savings banks, savings and loan associations, credit unions, and even the brokerage industry. At the time of this writing, these diversification efforts have already forced banking itself to change markedly, with even more changes on the horizon. It remains for future writers to relate whether efforts at diversification by these other institutions lead to their later retreat back to fundamentals in the way banking's era of aggressive growth ended.

All these changes are reflected in this new, third edition. Two new chapters have been added to cover the recent ways in which banking and its competitors have changed. But the basic purposes of the book—an examination of the role played by the banking industry as a link between credit control and economic activity and the understanding of what banking is as a business—have remained unaltered.

If anything, over time the link between the effectiveness of Federal Reserve operations and economic activity has been made even more dependent upon the actions and policies of the banking industry. As the author attempts to show, we can study the Fed and what it wants to do, but the Fed's role as the *hammer* on the economy is strictly limited by the response of the *anvil*—the commercial banking industry and the other financial institutions subject to the impact of credit control by the Federal Reserve. Since the first volume appeared, this role of middleman between the Fed and the economy has increased in importance because of the innovative ways in which many banks and thrift institutions have tried to alter the impact of credit control so that, despite Federal Reserve restraint, they could continue to serve their customers.

The response of the Fed itself and of Congress and the other regulators—entering more than ever before in bank policy determination and credit allocation—is a topic only touched on in this book, because it is the basis of what is likely to occur in the future. But it is hoped that this volume can help explain why all the players in the game of credit control and credit allocation are working so hard at defending their present positions while at the same time jockeying for more power in the financial environment.

The author's gratitude to those listed in the preface to the first edition remains unchanged. The author continues to add his deep appreciation to his wife, Ruth, for her help and encouragement in this, as well as in all other, endeavors. He would also like to thank his four children, Julie, Margaret, David, and Saul, for making the completion of this and all other professional work a true challenge.

Summit, N.J.   P.S.N.
February 1978

Preface to the First Edition

Commercial banking as a business is given fairly short shrift in the education of most students. Although credit creation and the role of the Federal Reserve System receive considerable attention, generally the operations and functions of the commercial banks are covered only briefly.

The role of the banks is a crucial one in credit control. They serve as the middlemen between the Federal Reserve and the economy, transmitting the pressures of restraint when money is made tight and aggressively pursuing potential borrowers when credit becomes easy. Yet few students gain real comprehension of what motivates the banks and how they perform their role of middlemen between credit-policy decisions and economic activity.

This method of credit control, though, is by no means the most effective way of controlling the business cycle and of furthering sustainable economic growth. Far more efficient and effective control could be exercised if people were willing to have their spending, saving, and investing policies directed for them by the government. The major virtue of the credit-control process that the United States has evolved is that the government's role is minimal; it is the commercial banks that perform the major tasks of allocating funds among potential borrowers when restraint is needed and of inducing borrowing and spending when the economy needs new stimulation. Our present credit-control structure, then, is not the most efficient, but rather happens to be the most compatible within a framework of freedom.

One might worry about the implications of having the banking industry play so significant a role in the economy, since this gives it an inordinate potential power of influencing economic activity. But the commercial banking system does not look upon itself as a seat of power for economic control. It operates as a group of business enterprises, each dedicated to earning the maximum profit compatible with the safety of its depositors' and stockholders' funds. Thus it is profit maximization under conditions of reasonable prudence that motivates the banker, rather than his power to control economic activity.

The banks' control over fund allocation is no more than an instinctive by-product of the prime bank function of profit maximization. The decisions of who receives money when credit is tight and of where loans will be aggressively solicited when credit is easy are simply reflex actions in the banker's effort to operate a profitable business, rather than an attempt by the banker to use his special role as a means of exerting strong influence on the social or economic fabric of the nation. This is why an understanding of banking as a business and of the banker's motivation becomes so necessary a prerequisite to full understanding of how monetary policy actually affects the economy.

It must be recognized, of course, that the question of transmission of Federal Reserve policy to the economy through the commercial banks is an extremely significant one, and that the nature and effectiveness of this transmission, or "linkage" process, are receiving considerable study at the present time.

This book is not aimed at expanding our theoretical knowledge in this linkage area. It is an attempt to use the transmission, or linkage, theme as a means of providing a better understanding of the role of the Federal Reserve and the banking system to both college students and those whose occupations can be made more meaningful by a better understanding of our financial environment.

Commercial Banking in the Economy was originally suggested by Professor Harlan M. Smith, of the University of Minnesota, as part of the Random House series in Money and Banking. I thank Professor Smith for his invitation to participate in the series and for his help in preparing this study. I also owe a deep debt of gratitude to Martin Blyn, William Freund, Michele Jarmak, Robert Kavesh, Rose Kestenbaum, Mordecai Rosenfeld, Arnold Sametz, and Thomas O. Waage for their encouragement and help in the preparation of the manuscript.

New York City   P.S.N.
February 1968

Contents

COMMERCIAL
BANKING
in the
ECONOMY

1

The Role of Financial Institutions and Markets

An understanding of the role of commercial banks and other financial institutions might well commence with a brief discussion of the circular flow of funds through the economy.

As Figure 1 illustrates, the available supply of money, which for this purpose can be simply defined as currency and deposits in checking accounts, or demand deposits, discharges its economic function by moving in a circle. The money flows from producing units to consuming units, because the consumers work for the producers and are paid with money, and then it flows back from the consuming units to the producers as payment for the goods and services the producers have produced.

We will make the clarifying assumptions that the consuming units are all family households and the producing units are all factories and the other producers who employ the breadwinners of these families. For purposes of simplicity we can ignore the fact that producing units are also consumers of some goods and services and no black-and-white separation of producers and consumers is possible.

This simple scheme of the circular flow of funds in the economy, while omitting much detail, does show that as long as the consumers spend all they earn on new goods and services produced by the producers, and as long as the producers pay out all their receipts to consuming units—either in salaries or in profits—our economy will function at a steady pace, and no cyclical problems will develop.

But such a simple monetary flow cannot exist for long. In the first place, there is a natural desire to save. It is hard to envision a group of consumers all of whom wish to spend every last cent

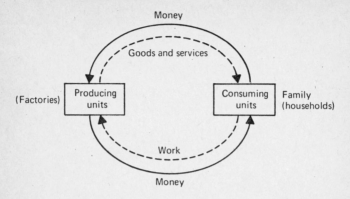

Figure 1   Circular Flow of Funds in the Economy

they earn. Someone or some group of people is bound to want to reduce spending below maximum income to save some money for future use or for a rainy day. Yet, as our simple flow-of-funds model is constituted, such a decision to save would immediately have repercussions on our economic environment; if even one person desires to save part of his or her income and not to spend it, there is less money in the spending stream. Then, in the next time period, demand for the products of producers is reduced, and since producers now earn less, they must reduce the money they pay out to the household units in salaries and profits. Thus, in the same way that a car with one leaky piston would slowly lose all its oil, an economy with some savers would slowly decline in vitality (at least until it reached the point at which people's incomes became so low that they could no longer afford the luxury of saving), unless there were some way of replacing the saved money in the spending stream.

This replacement is in fact what does occur when people save. Instead of being placed in a mattress or being privately hoarded in some other way, most of the saved money moves into the hands of borrowers—those who want to spend more than they have earned. And, as Figure 2 shows (again using the simplifying assumption that all borrowing is done by producing units), as long as borrowers are willing and able to borrow and spend the full amount that the savers desire to save, our economy continues to move along at a steady pace. In this regard, the saving-borrowing process is like a lateral pass that keeps the football moving when the first runner faces tacklers ahead of him. The meeting place of savers and borrowers is called the *money market* for short-term funds and the *capital market* for longer-term funds.

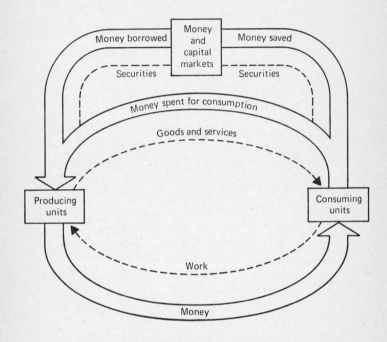

Figure 2   Circular Flow of Funds Including Savings and Borrowings

The process of saving and borrowing appears simple enough, and yet it is subject to more misconceptions than almost any other aspect of economics. Although most people have a full understanding of the role of saving and feel that the process of saving is good for both the individual and the economy, a great many people feel that debt is bad. Rising debt is frequently regarded as a sign of improvidence, and the fact that America's debts—both governmental and private—continue to grow makes many feel that our economy is headed for disaster. Yet slightly closer examination reveals that this rising debt is a necessary corollary of a rising volume of savings; without growth in our debts, the money that people desire to save would be hoarded instead of being recirculated into the spending stream, and the level of economic activity would have to be reduced by the amount of this increase in the hoarded money. Thus it should be firmly kept in mind that there is nothing inherently wrong with debt. Rather, an economy's debts must rise to match the growth in its savings.

What must be prevented is not debt itself but unmanageable debt—an amount of debt so large relative to the borrower's earning power that it threatens his ability to meet the interest payments and to repay the principal when it is due. Private debt can grow and still remain manageable as long as the borrower's income grows rapidly enough for interest payments and principal repayments to be no undue burden on his standard of living. Similarly, a governmental unit can increase its debts as long as its revenue potential from tax collections and other sources is large enough to cover debt service and principal repayments without subjecting the populace to unduly high taxes. A growing economy can support growing debt just as an individual can whose income is rising.

Without debt, our economy would be as vulnerable as the car with the leaky piston, because our economic stability would depend upon our ability to discourage virtually all savings. Equally significant, when debt is incurred to obtain productive facilities —be these investments in the form of machines, education, or health—ultimately this debt helps the economy grow; the person who borrows to invest in new productive equipment or to get an education expects that his earning power will be increased as the result of his investment, and the growth in each person's earning power is an intrinsic part of a nation's economic growth. For these two basic reasons, then, economic growth would be far more difficult to achieve without debt.

The Intermediation Process

How are funds actually transferred from savers to borrowers? In its simplest form, the transfer consists of the saver meeting the borrower and lending him his excess funds. Because there are a vast number of individual savers and borrowers, however, it is difficult for the individual saver to know who is in the market to borrow his money and what is the credit standing of the potential borrower. Similarly, potential borrowers have no way of knowing which individual savers have funds available; furthermore, even if they did know who wanted to invest, they would find it cumbersome and prohibitively expensive to gather the small amounts each saver has available in order to accumulate the amount needed. To perform these functions, advanced economies develop organized money and capital markets.

The organized money and capital markets consist of an informal structure of securities dealers who provide a means by which potential borrowers of large sums sell bonds and other debt securities to potential investors. An artificial distinction is drawn by which the dealing in securities that come due within a year comprises the money market and the structure for trading in longer-term obligations comprises the capital market. The same principles of operation hold for both; the only real distinction between them is the maturity structure of the obligations traded.

A bond issue is really nothing more than a large loan broken up into small, uniform certificates representing participations in the loan. By this method the borrower who sells bonds in the capital market can attract the savings of many individuals, because his issue is large enough to be bought by securities dealers, who publicize it and aggressively seek buyers among the nation's savers. The size of the issue is large enough also to make it worthwhile for the borrower to provide considerable information for the public on his credit standing, his earning power, and thus on his ability to meet interest and principal payments while, in many instances, the law requires such information to be available to potential investors. This provides the individual saver with a way of finding out who potential borrowers of his money are and what the quality of their financial standing is. Thus, the organized money and capital markets provide an alternative to direct contact between potential borrowers and those holding savings they wish to invest, serving as intermediaries between the two.[1]

---

[1] In the United States, the organized stock markets—such as the New York Stock Exchange—do not serve the primary function of bringing together borrowers and lenders, and thus have a function different than the organized money and capital

But the organized money and capital markets are not the outlet for all, or even the bulk of, potential borrowing. As the statistics on sources and uses of net new funds in Table 1 indicate, the largest single user of borrowed funds virtually every year—the residential mortgage—as well as all consumer borrowing and much business borrowing consists of amounts too small to make it worthwhile to float a bond issue on the organized money or capital market. Some other means, therefore, must be found to bring together these potential borrowers of small amounts and the savers who have funds to invest.

Some of this money is provided directly by the savers, because there are individuals and others who lend money to potential homeowners and other consumer borrowers. But the bulk of the funds that flow to the smaller borrowers is channeled through institutions that gather the savings of those who do not invest directly through the organized money and capital markets and then place these funds to work for the savers, lending much of them to individual borrowers.

To summarize, then, there are three basic ways in which the savings of an advanced economy can be channeled to the borrower.

1. By the direct meeting of money- and capital-market borrowers and lenders
2. Through the sale by the borrower in the organized money and capital markets of bonds and other public investment instruments, which in turn are bought directly by the savers
3. Through the use of financial institutions that gather the savings of individuals, place part of the proceeds directly into loans to other individuals, and assemble the rest into larger blocks of money, which are invested in securities sold on the organized money and capital markets.

Two basic types of institutions channel the public's savings into

---

markets. Although small amounts of bonds are traded on the New York Stock Exchange, trading on a stock exchange consists principally of the buying and selling of outstanding shares of stock, which represent the ownership of corporations. Instead of bringing borrowers and lenders together, a stock exchange provides a place for a holder of stock to get his money back by selling his holdings to a new buyer. Only when new stock is sold to the public by a corporation does the sale of stock absorb savings from the public.

Table 1 Summary of Sources and Uses of Funds ($ Billions)

	Annual Net Increases in Amounts Outstanding							Amounts Outstanding 12/31/77(e)
	1972	1973	1974	1975	1976	1977(e)	1978(p)	
Uses of Funds								
Privately Held Mortgages	68.8	68.7	42.8	40.2	72.0	94.0	97.0	866.4
Corporate Bonds	18.9	13.2	26.9	32.9	30.7	29.5	32.2	366.2
Domestically Held Foreign Bonds	1.0	1.0	2.2	6.2	8.4	4.3	4.0	37.5
Subtotal Long-Term Private	88.7	82.9	71.9	79.3	111.1	127.8	133.2	1,270.1
Business Loans	26.2	41.0	35.6	-12.4	5.4	34.1	43.5	277.0
Consumer Installment Credit	14.8	21.4	9.3	7.5	20.5	32.0	36.5	217.5
All Other Bank Loans	9.4	6.8	3.6	2.7	12.1	13.2	14.0	114.3
Open-Market Paper	1.6	8.3	17.7	-1.3	8.1	13.7	15.5	88.2
Subtotal Short-Term Private	52.0	77.5	66.2	-3.5	46.1	93.0	109.5	697.0
Privately Held Treasury Debt	16.0	-0.6	9.7	76.3	58.6	48.2	54.2	453.8
Privately Held Federal Agency Debt	11.5	22.2	19.7	11.5	16.9	24.4	30.0	163.5
Subtotal Federal	27.5	21.6	29.4	87.8	75.5	72.6	84.2	617.3
State & Local Tax-Exempt Bonds	14.1	13.3	11.9	17.5	21.7	30.4	23.2	260.9
State & Local Tax-Exempt Notes	-1.3	0.8	2.6	-1.2	-4.6	-0.7	-2.0	12.6
Subtotal Tax-Exempt	12.8	14.1	14.5	16.3	17.1	29.7	21.2	273.5
Total Net Demand for Credit	181.0	196.1	182.0	179.9	249.8	323.1	348.1	2,857.9

Sources of Funds[a]

Mutual Savings Banks	8.8	5.3	3.2	10.6	12.5	11.8	10.8	134.5
Savings & Loan Associations	35.3	27.1	19.6	37.4	50.5	60.5	57.4	410.8
Credit Unions	3.0	3.6	2.8	5.4	5.8	7.5	7.6	45.1
Life Insurance Companies	8.8	10.0	10.3	15.3	22.3	23.6	24.2	256.1
Fire & Casualty Companies	3.8	3.5	4.6	8.2	8.8	10.5	11.0	74.3
Private Noninsured Pension Funds	−0.7	2.0	5.8	7.9	5.3	10.2	11.4	67.0
State & Local Retirement Funds	3.1	3.4	8.0	8.3	9.6	10.9	11.2	95.1
Foundations & Endowments	−0.1	0.6	0.9	1.1	0.9	0.7	1.0	16.8
Closed-End Corporate Bond Funds	1.2	1.1	0.2	0.0	0.0	0.0	0.0	2.8
Money Market Funds	0.0	0.0	1.0	0.7	0.4	−0.3	0.5	1.9
Municipal Bond Funds	0.4	0.7	1.1	2.2	3.1	4.5	5.0	13.8
Open-End Taxable Investment Funds	0.0	−0.2	−0.4	0.8	1.1	1.1	0.3	9.6
Real Estate Investment Trusts	4.1	5.6	0.2	−4.9	−3.7	−1.5	−1.2	7.8
Finance Companies	9.4	11.6	4.9	1.3	8.7	19.9	20.0	122.5
Total Nonbank Institutions	77.1	74.3	62.2	94.3	125.3	159.4	159.2	1,258.1

Table 1 (Continued)

	1972	1973	1974	1975	1976	1977(e)	1978(p)	Amounts Outstanding 12/31/77(e)
			Annual Net Increases in Amounts Outstanding					
Commercial Banks^b	73.3	77.6	59.8	31.0	64.0	78.4	93.3	883.8
Business Corporations	-2.7	0.9	8.8	9.5	11.9	7.7	5.3	74.3
State & Local Governments	5.5	3.3	1.2	3.4	4.9	15.5	13.1	58.7
Foreigners	8.4	0.6	11.2	6.1	15.2	30.2	31.8	126.9
Subtotal	161.6	156.7	143.2	144.3	221.3	291.2	302.7	2,401.8
Residual: Households Direct	19.4	39.4	38.8	35.6	28.5	31.9	45.4	456.1
Total Net Supply of Credit	181.0	196.1	182.0	179.9	249.8	323.1	348.1	2,857.9

e Estimated in whole or in part.
p Projected.
^aExcludes funds for equities, cash, and miscellaneous demands not tabulated above.
^bIncludes loans transferred to books of nonoperating holding and other bank-related companies.

Source: Henry Kaufman and James McKeon, "Prospects for the Credit Markets in 1978." Monograph published by Salomon Brothers, New York, 1977.

loans and investments—commercial banks and financial interme- diaries. What distinguishes the intermediaries from commercial banks is that the former are basically just what they are called, intermediaries—conduits that channel the savings of the econ- omy into debt instruments of various types. They can lend only the amount they have received from savers, and, unlike the com- mercial banks, they cannot create new deposit money. In fact, the functioning of a financial intermediary is similar to that of an individual. An individual keeps his money either in the form of cash or in a commercial bank deposit. When he wants to lend money, all he can lend is his cash or the money he can obtain by writing a check. (An individual cannot lend the money he has in a savings account without first converting it either to cash or to a deposit in a checking account—he cannot give a borrower a piece of his passbook or otherwise spend savings in a savings account without first converting it to cash or to a demand deposit. This is why money in a savings account at a bank or a savings and loan association is called *near money,* to distinguish it from active spending money, i.e., the currency and demand deposits of the active money supply, which can be spent immediately.)

A financial intermediary, too, keeps its funds in cash or on deposit with a commercial bank, and it pays out most of its money by writing checks on commercial bank accounts, just as individu- als do when they want to spend or invest money without using cash.

A financial intermediary cannot create money. It can, as we shall discuss later, speed the velocity or turnover of demand de- posit money. When the individual saver writes a check on his checking account and places the funds with a financial intermedi- ary, the intermediary deposits the funds in its own checking ac- count. Then, when the financial intermediary lends out the funds, it does so by writing a check on its bank demand deposit account, and the money is deposited in the checking account of the home builder or other person who is borrowing the funds. Thus, the velocity of money is increased, and this in turn can have a major impact on economic activity. A faster rate of turnover of one sum of money can have the same impact on the economy as an in- creased quantity of money.

If the influence on velocity is ignored for the present, we see that financial intermediaries merely keep the circular flow of funds moving through the economy. They can do no more to increase economic activity than can be accomplished by savers putting their funds directly into the hands of borrowers.[2]

Commercial banks, on the other hand, can create money. As will be shown, when a commercial bank makes a loan, it actually creates new checking-account deposit money that did not exist before, unless the money borrowed is taken out in cash and remains as such. This procedure may appear mystifying now, but it should become clear later in the chapter. The ability of the bank to create money is the basic difference between a bank and a financial intermediary.

The fact that financial intermediaries cannot create money does not deny them importance in the circular flow of funds in the economy, as a brief description of each type of financial intermediary should indicate. But it must be remembered that financial intermediation is a process of bringing savers and borrowers together and, again ignoring the impact on velocity of money, it can do nothing to give the money supply flexibility.

The major forms of American financial intermediaries are listed and discussed below.

1. *Mutual savings banks.* Mutual savings banks are owned mutually by their depositors and either pay out their profits to savers in interest dividends or retain them as a reserve cushion against loss. These savings banks, about 500 in number, place their savers' funds largely in home mortgages and in small part into bonds of the federal government and other public and private borrowers in the organized money and capital markets. Because there are at this writing no federal laws enabling the chartering of mutual savings banks, they exist only in the eighteen states—mainly in the Northeast—that presently charter them.

---

[2]It must be noted that in a few states savings institutions are allowed to offer checking accounts, and in New England thrifts and commercial banks alike are authorized to offer NOW (Negotiable Order of Withdrawal) accounts, savings accounts on which checklike drafts may be written. Because the activity in these accounts is generally handled through checking accounts held by the thrift institutions at local commercial banks and because the amounts involved are still small, for clarity we still separate all accounts at thrift institutions from commercial bank checking accounts, calling all thrift institution deposits *near money* even if checks or drafts may be written on them.

2. *Savings and loan associations.* Although savings and loan associations are similar to mutual savings banks, there are two major differences. First, they were organized to obtain funds for home construction, so usually more of their savings are placed into home mortgages than is the case with mutual savings banks. Second, whereas in most states savings and loan associations are mutual organizations and thus divide their profits between their savers and their reserve fund, in a few states stock savings and loans are legal. In these institutions there is a layer of stockholders who receive those profits over and above what is paid out to savers and what must be retained to augment the cushion of reserves against loss. There are approximately 4,200 savings and loans associations, which are located in all states; some are federally chartered and others are chartered by their respective states.

3. *Credit unions.* Credit unions are mutual institutions whose membership has some common bond, such as employment in the same company. Members with available savings place them in the credit union, and the money is lent to other members who wish to borrow for such purposes as the purchase of homes and automobiles. The United States has about 22,500 credit unions.

4. *Insurance companies.* The prime motivation of people who place money in life insurance companies is not savings but insurance. If the insured person dies much earlier than normal life-expectancy tables predict, his family receives a return on its money well above what other forms of saving provide. This money is provided through the payment of a relatively lower return on the policyholders' investment to the beneficiaries of insured savers who live a longer life span than normal. Life insurance companies are both mutual and stockholder owned. Although the insurance feature differentiates insurance companies from other financial intermediaries, the function of both in the economy is similar. They receive funds from policyholders and place the funds in loans, both individually to home buyers and other small borrowers and also through security purchases in the organized money and capital markets.

In addition to life insurance companies there are also fire and casualty companies. These are technically not financial intermediaries; people invest money in them to buy protection against fire and other losses and not as a form of saving to protect their beneficiaries. As Table 1 shows, however, they are also a major force in the money and capital markets because of the investments they make with the premium dollars they hold as reserves to meet claims when they arise.

5. *Pension funds.* Pension funds are similar to insurance companies in that the saver, or his employer, or both place money into the fund and the amount received back is not exactly proportional to the amount saved but depends on the life span of the employee. The procedure for pension funds is the reverse of that for insurance companies. The person who lives the longest beyond retirement receives the highest return on his investment (through the periodic pension checks he receives); the person who dies before retirement and the person who dies relatively soon after retirement both receive lower returns on the money saved, unless a minimum number of payments have been guaranteed by insurance protection. In terms of economic role, the pension funds also invest directly and through the organized money and capital markets, as do insurance companies.

6. *Bond and money-market funds.* These are institutions that accept savings and place them in a pool for investment that allows diversification of assets. Instead of owning one bond or one money-market instrument, the saver owns a share of a fund that holds a variety of debt instruments, thus diversifying the saver's risk. (This is similar to a *mutual fund,* a vehicle that allows the saver to buy a share in a diversified portfolio of stocks instead of having to restrict his investment to one or a few selected issues.)

7. *Real estate investment trusts.* Real estate investment trusts are similar to mutual funds and bond funds. But instead of owning a diversified portfolio of bonds or stocks, the saver owns a share of a portfolio of mortgage loans or of actual real estate properties. This allows the saver to invest in real estate without having to take the risk of putting all his money in one or two projects.

Bond and money-market funds and real estate investment trusts are sold by regular stock and bond dealers, making it easier for the general public to invest than it would be if they had to select by themselves specific issues, mortgages, or real estate.

8. *Mortgage companies.* Mortgage companies are a somewhat different type of financial intermediary from the seven mentioned above. Instead of serving as an intermediary between the saver

and the organized capital market, or the saver and the borrower, the main function of such companies is to serve as an intermediary between the borrower and the other financial intermediaries. Mortgage companies are institutions that make mortgage loans in the territories where they are located. Unlike savings banks, savings and loan associations, insurance companies, pension funds, and credit unions, which lend money turned over to them by savers, mortgage companies do not seek the savings of the public. They take mortgages they have originated and sell them to other institutions in other regions (and sometimes in their own region) that have more savings than they have profitable lending outlets for. Mortgage companies also collect the interest and amortization payments for the ultimate lender. In this way they too serve a useful function in the process of bringing borrowers and lenders together.

9. *Finance companies.* Finance companies are also somewhat different in function from the first seven intermediaries discussed. The over 5,000 finance companies in the nation are divided into two types: (1) sales and personal finance companies, which make loans to individuals for such purposes as automobile purchase, and (2) commercial finance companies, which make loans to business firms. These business loans are generally secured by inventories or receivables, and are usually made to companies whose less attractive collateral and low capitalization entail enough risk to make commercial banks hesitate to grant them credit accommodation. Finance companies obtain their funds from three main sources: (1) their own stockholders' capital, (2) money borrowed from commercial banks, and (3) money obtained by selling securities on the organized money and capital markets. Through this third fund source, finance companies consolidate the small borrowings of their customers into units large enough to enable them to tap the organized money and capital markets just as the first seven types of institutions described consolidate small savings into units large enough to place as investments in the money and capital markets.

The assets of the commercial banks and of those financial intermediaries who also tap the public's savings (so that a comparison between them has some validity and usefulness) are estimated in the final column of Table 1.

The functions of the financial intermediaries mentioned above should give some idea of the significance of their individual roles and their combined importance in channeling savings into the hands of borrowers. But as has been stressed above, except for their impact on the speed of turnover of money, they can do nothing to augment the money supply.

Why is an augmented money supply ever needed? The answer is that if the economy is to expand, unless the velocity of money can expand indefinitely, the money supply, like the amount of debt, must not be maintained at some specific figure but must grow. As the productive capacity and manpower of an economy increase, the available spendable money must rise also, since money is the only efficient medium of exchange and universal standard of value. Otherwise a stable amount of money will be chasing a larger supply of goods and services, and a fall in prices will result.

Since we seem to live in a time of continual erosion of the value of money, a decline in the prices of goods and services may appear on the surface to be desirable to us, but on deeper examination such a deflation is seen to offer its own dangers to economic stability.

In a society in which prices continue to fall, there will be a natural hesitancy to spend if it is felt that the passage of time will reduce prices even further. This will be accompanied by a similar hesitancy to borrow and invest, because again the reward for delay would be lower costs and prices. The delays in spending and borrowing for investment bring with them a slowing down in the circular flow of funds, which in turn brings a recession, unemployment of men and productive capacity, and still lower prices.

Equally important, a society with a static money supply finds it extremely difficult to develop new productive capacity. One of the basic ways in which new capital goods are financed is through the creation of new money that is lent to the builder of these facilities. Since the newly created money brings forth expanded capacity of the economy, and thus an increase in physical output, it does not bid up the cost of living, because a rise in goods available will develop to match the rise in money supply.

A static money supply would bring about recessionary tendencies, if the economy were to try to expand physically, while also serving as a deterrent to that physical economic growth in the first place.

Put in its simplest terms, an economy of 200 million people needs more money supply than an economy of 100 million people.[3] Yet the circular flow-of-funds structure presented so far provides no means of increasing the money supply as the population expands or as the need for money otherwise increases.

To explain how the flexibility of money supply came about, it is often simplest to turn to the days of the medieval goldsmiths and examine their operations.

The goldsmiths in the Middle Ages served not only as artisans but also as trusted safekeepers of gold. People with gold would often deposit it with their goldsmith, taking home a receipt; and when they were in need of spending money, they turned in their receipts and took out gold. In time the tendency naturally developed to leave the gold with the goldsmith and simply spend the receipt, because usually a man paid in gold deposited the gold with the goldsmith in exchange for a receipt. Moreover, goldsmiths often lent out their own gold for interest, yet often this gold was deposited right back into their hands, the borrower taking and spending a certificate instead, because it was more convenient.

It was not long before some goldsmiths recognized that day after day, week after week, month after month, people exchanged gold for certificates, and other people turned in certificates for gold, but at the end of every day there were always some certificates outstanding and some gold in the vault.

Then undoubtedly the day came when a customer came to the goldsmith to borrow gold, but the goldsmith had lent all his own gold and had available only gold deposited with him for safekeeping. The goldsmith must have thought, "Here is a chance to lend out some gold. It isn't mine, but people continually spend my certificates rather than gold, and I always have some gold left at the end of every day, why not lend some of the other people's gold

[3]Whether the money supply must grow at the same rate as the economy is one of the heated questions of today. Some economists say that it must; others, including the author, feel that no exact relationship between expansion of money supply and expansion of the economy is necessary, because of the important role that speeded turnover of money can play in helping finance economic growth

that is here? Since not everyone wants his gold at the same time, and since every piece looks alike, so no one knows which gold was originally his, who's to know if I have more certificates outstanding than I have gold?"

And at that moment, the first bank was born.

Depositor Confidence

The above story illustrates the two features that empower the bank to create money:

1. The bank must gain the confidence of the public so that people not only want to leave their currency and metallic money with it but also will find claims on the bank acceptable as spending money. In the goldsmiths' day, the reason that receipts were used for money was that they were accepted by people in payment for purchases. What makes a bank demand deposit into money today is that we will accept a check—which is really only an order to a banker telling him to pay a certain person a specific sum—as payment for debts. Anyone can try to pay a debt by offering a piece of paper that says a third party should give a specific sum to the payee, but only when that third party is a bank do we accept the piece of paper as money.

2. There must be people who wish to borrow money. It must not be forgotten that the goldsmith could not create money until someone wished to borrow from him. He could create all the certificates he wanted, but until there was a borrower, it was impossible for the outstanding certificates to exceed his available supply of gold.

It is this very power to create money when people desire to borrow it that makes our money supply flexible. People borrow only when they need to. If the amount that people want to borrow exceeds the amount that others have saved, the power of the banks to create the additional money enables the growth of the money supply to match the rise in spending desires. Without the banks' ability to create new money as it is desired, potential borrowing and spending in excess of available savings would have to be denied, and the rate of spending in the economy could not grow.

To be sure, there can be disadvantages, too, in a flexible money supply, as will be shown later, but for the time being the point that needs attention is how the banks create money, rather than the potential good or evil inherent in this power.

The goldsmith created money by having more certificates outstanding than he had gold in the vault. Because people kept and spent his certificates as the equivalent of gold, his action increased the money supply.

Similarly, a modern bank creates new money if, when it lends money, people are willing to hold their money in demand deposit form instead of demanding currency. One might at first question the assumption that people will keep the money as a demand deposit instead of converting it to cash. Yet empirical evidence shows that the amount of currency in circulation does not fluctuate as widely as the amount of checkbook money, and that over 90 percent of the volume of transactions is financed by checks on demand deposits instead of by cash.

More specifically, a bank can lend money in three ways: by crediting the customer's checking account, by writing a cashier's check, and by paying out cash. All three will increase the money supply, unless the public increases its desire to hold currency.

When a bank makes a loan to a business firm, it usually simply credits the customer's checking account once the loan is approved, so that the customer can then buy whatever he wanted the borrowed funds for and can pay by check. The assumption—based on the financial habits of the American people—is that the recipient of this check also places it in a checking account instead of demanding cash.

If the customer is paid with a cashier's official check, as in the case of a person borrowing money to buy a house, the likelihood again is that when the money reaches its ultimate recipient, the seller of the house, he will deposit it and increase the size of his demand deposit account. Since the cashier's check itself is merely a piece of paper until the bank officer signs it and turns it over to the borrower, bank demand deposits are increased by this borrowing transaction, because a new demand deposit has been created through the issuing and subsequent deposit of one official check.

Finally, even if the borrower wants currency, it is likely that his loan will increase demand deposits and thus the money supply. The borrower undoubtedly wants to spend his proceeds, and the recipient of the currency will probably prefer to deposit it and increase his bank account rather than to keep the cash on hand. The cash will return to the banking system, and yet new demand deposit money will have been created with the proceeds of the loan.

It should be obvious by now that the effective functioning of the banking system depends upon the willingness of people to leave deposits in the bank.

If all the people holding certificates issued by a goldsmith had wanted their gold at a time when he had issued more certificates than he had gold, there would have been one embarrassed, bankrupt, and discredited goldsmith. Similarly, when a banker gains new deposits, he counts on the depositors' leaving it with him, and so lends most of it out at interest. He also counts on the fact that if the person making the deposit withdraws his money later, either by writing a check that is deposited in another bank or by taking out cash, by the law of averages someone else will at the same time deposit new cash into his bank or deposit a check written on a different bank, and so make up this loss. The banker maintains some reserve funds for times when the law of averages fails him, and he also knows that in this country the Federal Reserve System—the banker's bank—will help him out with money for short periods when the fund outflow is beyond his control. But basically the banker counts on the law of averages, and except for the Federal Reserve System, a relatively recent development, he is just as unable to cope with a large-scale loss of depositor confidence and demand for cash as was the goldsmith with more certificates outstanding than gold on hand.

This is what makes a bank-run so dangerous. A "run on a bank" results from the loss of confidence by depositors in an individual bank or in several banks such that a great many of them demand withdrawal of their money at once. The bulk of demand deposits has been created through the making of loans and investments, and since most of a bank's assets consist of these loans and investments and not of vault cash, it is obvious that banks do not have enough cash to meet all claims at once. In fact, even of the money deposited in currency form, the banks keep only a small amount as actual cash. They find it useless to keep more cash than they need to meet normal cash withdrawals, plus what they are required to keep by law and regulation; as keeping cash on hand involves the sacrifice of the interest that could be earned by lending this money out.

Thus, banks require the confidence of their depositors and are highly vulnerable to a loss of confidence. This explains why in 1933 the United States established the Federal Deposit Insurance Corporation (FDIC) to insure bank deposits. If the public knows that deposits are insured by the federal government, the banks will not suffer the loss of confidence that leads to bank-runs and the consequent failure of all but the strongest and most liquid institutions.

Yet although most banks are protected from the contingency of runs by FDIC insurance of deposits, and although bankers know that the Federal Reserve will help them out temporarily if they suffer an unexpected demand for currency or an adverse movement of deposits from one bank to others, such protection does not relieve the banker of his responsibility to maintain enough cash and liquid assets to meet normal demands for funds and to handle greater than normal outflows without help most of the time. The banker recognizes that his survival is based on the confidence the public has in his institution, and that this in turn depends on his ability to operate a bank which has sound loans and also can meet all deposit outflows as they occur. He must constantly maintain a high standard in the quality of his assets, and considerable liquidity so as to be able to meet withdrawal requests from customers.

Meeting such standards, however, is expensive. A banker knows that high-quality loans offer lower interest returns than low-quality ones, whereas as a general rule investments and loans that are liquid—that is, quickly and readily convertible into cash without undue loss—offer lower yields than do less liquid assets. He must constantly face the dilemma of trying to maximize profits while keeping quality and liquidity strong, even though quality and liquidity can be obtained only at the expense of profitability. This is the basic internal struggle of the banking business. It is also the main force that determines how aggressive the banks are in lending and investing at any one time, and what types of loans and investments they are prepared to make.

This struggle is of key importance not only to the banks but also to the economy. For, as will be seen in the next chapter, our society has given to the commercial banks and to their lending and investing policies in particular the key role of transmitting to the marketplace the impact of governmental monetary controls placed over our economy

2

Credit Control

In the preceding chapter our concern was with how money is created by banks rather than with the pitfalls and promises inherent in this money-creating power.

It should be clear by now that a flexible money supply is needed if an economy wants sustainable economic growth. Throughout history lack of monetary flexibility has caused many a monetary panic, in addition to holding back advancement in the standard of living. Yet monetary flexibility is not without its drawbacks.

The basic problem in giving banks the ability to create a flexible money supply is that this power may well be abused. Certainly there is nothing wrong with banks creating money, as long as this creation is matched by a rise in the availability of goods and services. When this is the case, the rise in money supply matches the rise in goods and services on which the money can be spent, and there is no basic change upward or downward in the price level.

If the economy is underemploying its available manpower and productive facilities and a banker makes a loan that creates new money, this is all to the good, because the money borrowed undoubtedly was borrowed to be spent. As long as the circular flow of funds is not fast and strong enough to utilize all available workers and productive facilities, the infusion of additional money into the economy should do nothing but improve this utilization. The chance that additional spending power will bid up the price level when the economy has considerable excess capacity is zero in theory and small in practice.

However, if the economy is operating close to capacity of manpower and material and a bank makes a loan that increases the money supply, then the impact of this new spending power can be only to bid up the cost of living and to develop inflationary pressures. If you increase the money supply when the economy is unable to increase its output of goods and services for sale proportionately, all that the monetary increase can possibly do, aside from redirecting production, is increase the cost of those goods and services that are available.

Is there any reason why an individual bank might restrict its creation of money to the limit compatible with economic growth and a stable currency? The answer is no. The individual bank desiring to maximize profits concerns itself with whether the customer who wants to borrow money is creditworthy and whether the money will be returned with proper interest added. A single bank does not consider whether a loan will help the economy or hurt it, even assuming it has enough knowledge to determine what the loan's impact on the economy will be. Furthermore, the bank would have every reason to believe that if it suspected that a loan might hurt the economy and consequently refused it, another of the nation's 14,400 banks would make the loan and earn the profit it had denied itself.

While the banks' power to create money is a vital necessity for a growing economy, if it is not regulated it can also be a basic source of economic instability.

The banks' power to create money (and conversely to destroy it when loans are paid off) automatically makes them a natural medium for helping to regulate the business cycle, if the timing of their credit creation and credit destruction is skillfully handled.

In its rudiments, the business cycle develops because of the erratic timing of people's and business firms' desire to spend and invest. If the circular flow of funds were always smooth—the money that some people wish to save always just being absorbed by the borrowings of those who desire to spend more than they earn at the moment—the business cycle would not exist. To be sure, there would be no periods of rapid economic growth, but there would be no recession either, as long as the available manpower and productive capacity remained the same.

The immediate cause of the business cycle, then, is absence of equilibrium in monetary supply and demand. For a number of natural, technological, psychological, and economic reasons, at certain times the monetary requirements of the people who are borrowing and spending are well below the amounts that others are saving. Since the amount of money flowing through the economy falls when the amount saved exceeds the amount borrowed to spend and invest in new facilities, the economy suffers a decline that puts men out of work and leaves productive facilities unemployed. Conversely, when the desire of borrowers to spend and invest exceeds the available new savings, there is upward pressure on the economy, provided the borrowers can obtain the funds they want by borrowing from banks (thus creating new money), by tapping funds previously hoarded, or by speeding the turnover of the available money. Yet if this money is borrowed and spent at a time when the economy is operating at or close to capacity, then along with gaining some economic growth, the nation also experiences inflation.

The business cycle is caused by the psychology of the nation's spenders, the timing of technological developments that lead to new spending, and forces such as crop failures and natural disasters that determine when and how much people borrow, spend, hoard, and save. Yet many of these forces are beyond the control of the government, unless it can change tax policies drastically or is willing to interfere severely with the freedom of the individual and of the economy.

Yet the banks' ability to create and destroy money can play a major role in the control of the business cycle within a framework of freedom, if the banks' actions can be properly timed.

If the banking system can be influenced to restrict its lending and investing at times when the economy is at capacity and any new creation of money will bring inflation, the potential borrowers of funds can be discouraged in two ways—through higher interest rates and through diminished availability of funds.

The rate of interest that borrowers pay and lenders earn is determined by supply of and demand for funds. Assuming no international flow of capital, the rate of interest is determined, on the supply side, mainly by the amount of current saving (coupled with the amount formerly hoarded as cash and now being dishoarded) and the amount by which the money supply increases; and on the demand side, by hoarding, dissaving (or financing consumption from previously accumulated balances), and investment (which includes governmental deficit finance, money borrowed by business, and money borrowed by individuals for consumption spending over and above what they earn).

If the banking system can be induced to reduce its creation of new money, the supply of funds available to meet demands will be reduced, and consequently interest rates will rise. The rise in interest rates will discourage some borrowing and spending, especially by potential home buyers and home builders and state and local governments, and so some of the pressure for higher prices that an economy at capacity would otherwise feel will be relieved. While high interest rates discourage some borrowers, there are other potential borrowers whose fund demands are less sensitive to interest rate levels, notably business borrowers who expect to earn far more from the project for which they want to borrow money than the money will cost them, and consumers who pay more attention to the monthly payments they must make on the car or appliance they want to buy than to the rate of interest they must pay. But even these potential borrowers can be prevented from borrowing and spending if the ability of the banks to create new money can be curtailed. Although the potential borrowers will not be discouraged by the interest rate itself, if the banks can be prevented from creating new money at a time when savings and dishoarding do not equal total demands for funds, these borrowers will simply be unable to obtain the money they want.

Higher interest rates and restricted availability of funds both develop if the banks can be prevented from increasing the money supply. And both these restraining forces can help relieve the pressure on the economy at a time when the economy is close to capacity.

Conversely, if the banks can be induced to increase the money supply at times when the economy is underutilizing its capacity, this can help pull the nation out of a recession and help avoid the serious problem of unemployment. Again, it is the combined force of interest rates and availability that helps spur economic activity, if the banks can be induced to find borrowers and thus increase the money supply. The increased availability of funds presses downward on interest rates and also makes the holders of all lendable funds more aggressive and imaginative in trying to place their available funds at work, all of which spurs new borrowing and spending in the economy.

Thus, control over the banks' power to create money can accomplish two things: (1) it can avoid the pressures of inflation that would otherwise arise from unrestricted ability of the banks to expand the money supply whenever they found creditworthy potential borrowers; and (2) it can make the banks' money-creating power into a major tool for moderation of the business cycle without drastic interference in the free decision making of the economy.

The Control Mechanism

A simple solution has been developed to the problem of how to regulate the banks in their creation of money. The Congress simply requires that member banks must maintain a fractional reserve behind their demand and time deposits in the form of currency or deposits at the banker's bank—the Federal Reserve itself.

This process effectively limits the ability of the member bank to create new deposits. Unless the bank has excess cash on hand or money on deposit with the Federal Reserve over and above its legal requirement, legally it is not allowed to make a new loan or to buy a new investment, because by making these loans and investments it would be creating new demand deposits, which must be backed by reserves. Once a bank has created deposits up to the maximum allowable based on its available cash and deposits at the Federal Reserve, it cannot increase its loans and investments further, and thus cannot create new demand deposits. The only ways it can obtain new cash or deposits at the Federal Reserve are (1) by people bringing in cash for deposit, so as to reduce their total holdings of currency, (2) by people depositing money drawn from another bank, and (3) by the Federal Reserve allowing the bank to obtain new reserves through the means described below.

Yet if the Federal Reserve wants to restrict the ability of the banks to create money, none of these three possibilities can serve as an effective escape valve from the impact of reserve requirements. First, it is not likely that cash being deposited will provide much in the way of new reserves to the banking system, since the amount of currency held in circulation is fairly static in the short run. Second, if a bank obtains new reserves as a result of money flowing into it from another bank, its augmented ability to create new deposits will be offset by the reduced ability of the bank losing the money to support demand deposit creation. The movement of funds from one member bank of the Federal Reserve System to another takes place by the Federal Reserve reducing the deposit it holds for the bank on which the check is written and adding to the account of the bank receiving the check, just as an individual depositing a check in his account finds his bank balance increased at the expense of the balance of the writer of the check.

As for the third way of increasing the banks' power to create money (being allowed new reserves by the Federal Reserve), it is self-evident that if the Federal Reserve wants to restrict credit creation, it will do everything in its power to avoid giving the banks new reserves; and if new reserves are made available to the banks through forces beyond the Federal Reserve's control, it will sop these up through counteracting measures that absorb idle bank reserves.

The establishment of reserve requirements thus makes the banks' power to create money subservient to the wishes of the Federal Reserve System.

How does the Federal Reserve System change the reserve position of the banks so as to encourage them to lend at certain times and to restrict their lending powers at other times? This is accomplished principally through three powers: (1) altering reserve requirements, (2) changing the discount rate, and (3) open market operations.

Reserve requirement changes would be the simplest way of altering the banks' ability to make loans and so create new demand deposits. When the Federal Reserve wants to tighten credit, it could raise these requirements; when it wants to encourage more borrowing and spending, it could lower them. But this is a rather drastic move. Banks try to utilize all the lending power they have, and an aggressive bank always has its deposits right up to the maximum allowable based on available reserves.

When the Federal Reserve raises a bank's reserve requirements, such a bank would be forced to find new money or to reduce demand deposits in a hurry. The only avenues open to it would be the hurried sale of investments in a market flooded with the investments other banks are also trying to unload, the calling of loans, or the refusal to renew loans as they mature. It should be obvious that these would be drastic moves for banks to make, and certainly the customers whose loans were called or who found it impossible to renew loans on maturity would suffer markedly from such a procedure. So the Federal Reserve changes the reserve requirements only infrequently. It has gentler ways of achieving its aims.

Discount rate changes mean alteration in the rate of interest that the Federal Reserve charges member banks of the Federal Reserve System when they come to it to borrow money.

Why does the Federal Reserve System lend banks money? It must be remembered that banks rely on the law of averages in maintaining their deposit totals. However, it is impossible to be always correct in forecasting whether money will flow from your bank into currency in the public's hands or from your bank to other banks. If the individual banks were forced to keep enough cash on hand to meet all possible contingencies, they would have to sacrifice a good portion of their loans and investments. This would both hurt bank earnings severely and deny the public a substantial portion of the money it borrows from banks.

Thus the Federal Reserve stands ready to lend banks enough money to meet emergency needs for short periods, when deposit outflows are adverse and unexpected. It lets the bank borrow either with such securities as U.S. government bonds as collateral, which is called an advance, or by endorsing over the contracts for loans the bank has made to its customers, which is called *discounting* (but which has almost never been done for well over thirty years). The Federal Reserve lends by giving the bank a deposit in its account on the books of the Federal Reserve. This, of course, serves as a part of the bank's legally required reserves, and thus helps the bank offset the loss in currency or outflow of funds to other banks.

The rate the Federal Reserve charges for this credit accommodation is called the *rediscount* or *discount rate* (the terms are generally used interchangeably), although the term "rediscount rate" is disappearing since rediscounting of customers' notes virtually never occurs. When the Federal Reserve wants to tighten credit, one thing it can do is raise the rate it charges borrowing banks; conversely it can lower the rate when it wants to ease credit.

But, contrary to popular opinion, the discount rate itself is not a real force in making credit tighter or easier. Unlike the systems in most other countries, where the discount rate is a high, or "penalty," rate, the rate charged borrowing banks is usually well below what the banks can earn on loans and investments, so that a bank would be delighted to borrow from the Federal Reserve to cover a reserve deficiency if it could continue on its merry way without selling investments, reducing outstanding loans or restricting the granting of new loans. A rise in the discount rate of, say, 0.5 percent by itself would do little to discourage borrowing on the part of the banks; on the other hand, a decline in the rate would not encourage more bank borrowing. In fact, borrowings are always highest when the rate is highest, and vice versa.

Generally, what limits the amount of discounting is not the level of the rate, but rather the Federal Reserve's care in extending credit to banks through its discount window (as the process of borrowing from Federal is described). Discounts are usually for short time periods, and the Federal Reserve makes sure that banks use the privilege for meeting temporary reserve deficiencies and not as a way of obtaining enough new reserves in a period of tight money to carry on business as usual. "Borrowing from the Federal Reserve is a privilege and not a right," Federal Reserve officials frequently repeat. It is the availability of funds from the Federal Reserve that is the truly significant controlling mechanism, while the discount rate by itself is not of great importance in restricting or encouraging bank borrowing.

What, then, is the role of a change in the rediscount, or discount, rate? More than anything else, its function is a signal of Federal Reserve intentions as to whether it will be making credit tighter or easier. When the Federal Reserve raises the discount rate, it is a signal that money will be kept or made tighter. When it is lowered, most likely credit easing is on the way.

But if the discount rate change itself is only a signal and if changes in reserve requirements are infrequent, what mechanism does the Federal Reserve use to control the reserve positions of the banks and so control credit conditions in the economy? The answer is its open market operations.

Open market operations consist of the Federal Reserve's purchase and sale of U.S. government securities and other instruments in the organized money and capital markets. These transactions are made in the open market, the Federal Reserve selling to and buying from anybody, not only the commercial banks.

There is nothing especially significant about the fact that the Federal Reserve usually deals in U.S. government securities in its open market operations. As a matter of fact, it could deal in cases of beer or any other commodity. The significant fact is that it buys *something* when it desires to pump money into the economy and sells *something* when it desires to tighten credit.

What makes the Federal Reserve's open market operations effective is that when it buys, whether government securities or something else, it pays the seller with a cashier's check on itself. If the seller of the securities happens to be a bank, the bank deposits this check in its account at Federal, thus increasing its reserves and its lending power. If the seller happens to be someone other than a bank, he will deposit the check in his commercial bank, and in turn the bank will deposit the check with the Federal Reserve. In both cases the bank gets new reserves at Federal, which can be used to back new loans and so create new demand deposits.

The basic difference between the Federal Reserve's buying a security from a bank and from a nonbank is this: If a bank sells the security, it gets the full amount of the Reserve Bank's check as new reserves that can be used to back new demand deposits; if a nonbank gets the check and it deposits the check with a bank, the bank gets the same amount of new reserves when it deposits the check with Federal, but it cannot use all the receipts to back new demand deposit creation, because along with the Reserve Bank's check, the bank gets a new deposit from the seller of the securities, and a portion of the new reserves that the bank receives must be used to back this new deposit. Assuming reserve requirements are 20 percent and the amount of securities sold to Federal is $100, the bank will have $100 of new reserves in any case. If the bank itself sells the securities, all of that $100 will be what is called *excess reserves*, money free to back new creation of loans and deposits, provided that the bank has no reserve deficiency or borrowing to pay off. However, if the securities are sold by someone other than a bank and the $100 is then deposited in a bank, that bank will still get $100 of new reserves when it deposits the check in its own account at the Federal Reserve, but of that $100, $20 will be called *required reserves,* because it has to be maintained to back the new $100 deposit the bank received. Only $80 will be considered excess reserves, which the bank can use to back creation of new deposits.

In sum, if the Federal Reserve wants to ease credit in the banking system, it can buy securities and thus provide new bank reserves. Conversely, if the Federal Reserve wants to tighten credit, it sells securities. If banks buy them, they pay the Federal Reserve by having their deposits at Federal reduced, which lessens bank reserve positions. If the securities are bought by other than commercial banks (which includes all financial intermediaries), the Federal Reserve is paid by a check on the buyer's commercial bank; and when the Federal Reserve receives this check it deducts the amount from the account at Federal of the security buyer's commercial bank, reducing this bank's reserves.

Open market operations are conducted continually, and they serve as the main means available to the Federal Reserve of day-to-day control over the bank reserve positions and thus over the volume of credit extended in the economy.[1]

Fiscal Policy and Debt Management

Although *monetary policy,* the Federal Reserve's control over the reserve positions of the commercial banks, is one of the main

[1]The ability to control bank reserve positions on a day-to-day basis is important for effective credit control, because there are forces affecting bank reserve positions beyond the control of the Federal Reserve authorities. For example, if an individual deposits in his bank cash that formerly was in circulation, the bank can use this cash as a reserve and thus can expand loans, even though the Federal Reserve might want credit to remain stable or to contract at that time.

But while the Federal Reserve can do nothing to prevent the individual from depositing his excess cash and giving the bank new reserves, it can sop up an equivalent amount of reserves from the banking system through open market operations, thus neutralizing the impact of this cash deposit on the banking system's ability to create credit.

means of regulating the economy and controlling the business cycle in a framework of freedom, there are also two other major indirect means of economic control: *fiscal policy* of the Congress and *debt management policy* of the Treasury.

Fiscal policy can be defined as the Congressional decision as to how much the government will spend on what, and how much and what kind of taxes will be collected. (Of course, neither can be determined exactly, but spending can be fairly well approximated, while the level of tax rates provides a fair indicator of what revenue the federal government will receive.)

If the Congress is anxious to encourage spending in the economy, so as to pull the nation out of a recession, it can decide to operate with a deficit and spend more than it collects in taxes. Conversely, to reduce the pressures of inflation caused by spending power in excess of available goods and services, Congress can reduce the nation's ability to spend by collecting in taxes more than the government spends for goods and services.

In sum, deficit spending can stimulate an economy, while operating with a fiscal surplus can help reduce economic activity and thereby help control inflationary pressures.

However, an examination of surplus and deficits alone does not give a full picture of how fiscal policy works. If the government spends more than it collects in taxes, the extra money must come from somewhere. If the government operates with a surplus, something must happen to that money sopped out of the economy. The answer to this question involves the introduction of debt management.

Debt management is the decision of the Treasury as to how to finance the debt when the Congress has authorized more expenditure than tax rates collect. If the Treasury sells securities and they are bought and held by individuals and financial intermediaries, and not by the commercial banks and the Federal Reserve, then debt management can minimize the impact of deficit spending on the economy. For though the government is spending more than it is collecting in taxes, the additional money has been absorbed from the public anyway, the Treasury having borrowed money that people could otherwise spend. To be sure, when the Treasury borrows the money it needs instead of taxing it away, there will be a difference in the economic impact later, since the borrowed funds will some day be returned to the lenders, whereas taxpayers receive only fond or unfond memories of previous tax payments.

Current spending is likely to be increased to an unmeasurable degree when the government raises money by selling bonds instead of raising taxes, because the holders of the new bonds will feel wealthier than they would have felt with higher tax collections, and because of this many will spend more on current consumption than they would have done. But otherwise the immediate impact is the same when the Treasury sells more bonds to individuals and financial intermediaries and when taxes are raised.

Such similarity in impact, however, is not the case when the deficit is financed by selling the newly issued securities to the Federal Reserve or to a commercial bank that has excess reserves available; both these institutions can pay for securities by creating money. If the economy is suffering from inflationary pressures and the Treasury sells securities of the types bought by banks, the inflationary pressures will be intensified. The banks will pay for the securities by increasing the amount of demand deposit money chasing goods and services at a time when the economy is already suffering from an excess of money relative to available goods and services. On the other hand, if the securities are sold to individuals, or even to financial intermediaries, since neither can create money, the securities must be paid for by utilizing money already in existence, money that would otherwise by spent or loaned out. Thus, although there is no way in which debt management can make deficit spending an anti-inflationary weapon, it can neutralize the impact of deficit finance by gathering the funds to meet the deficits without resorting to the sale of securities to banks and thereby resorting to the creation of new money.

Conversely, if there is a surplus in the budget and the Treasury arranges that the securities retired are those of the banks, the money supply will decrease because, although banks make loans and pay for securities by creating new deposits, when loans or securities are retired these deposits are extinguished.

Such a reduction in the money supply through debt management can be of great value in helping reduce inflationary pressures. On the other hand, if there is a surplus at a time when the economy is underutilizing its capacity, then retirement of bank-held securities is poor policy, since the Treasury does not want to see the money supply reduced during a period of recession. At such a time the proper debt management policy for the Treasury is to try to have the securities that are retired be those of individuals, financial intermediaries, and other nonbank holders. The payment then received by these securities holders becomes available for spending or investing again, thus helping maintain spending. A reduction in the money supply would have reduced spending.

There is no way in which the Treasury can make a fiscal surplus into a weapon for economic expansion, but it can make it a neutral force or a contracting force, depending upon what is needed, by proper handling of debt management.

In practice, debt management is not as clear-cut as the above examples would indicate. If a bank has no excess reserves available, it cannot buy new Treasury securities without reducing other loans and investments, so no increase in the money supply can occur. If bank-held debt is retired and the banks then use the freed reserves to back new loans and investments, the contracting influence of the debt retirement is neutralized.

The result is that proper debt management is less of a problem in a boom than on other occasions. In a boom, many banks will be out of excess reserves and will not be able to buy government securities and thereby create new deposits, even if the type of securities the Treasury sells is in the maturity range that banks buy. But in recessions, if bank-held debt is retired, it may be hard for the bank to find new lending opportunities, so that if bank-held securities are retired, the bank may just sit with its excess reserves instead of using them to back new deposit creation. This does not negate the basic principles of debt management, however, and also, as will be seen later, debt management has decided economic impact through its effect on liquidity in the economy too.

The details of how debt management works must be reserved for later in this book, but one point should be clear from the start. Just as the banks are the middlemen between Federal Reserve monetary policy and the public's decisions to borrow and spend, the purchase and sale of government securities by the banks and the timing of these transactions play a key role in the effective handling of debt management; and proper debt management is a prerequisite for effective fiscal policy. Thus the commercial banks truly serve as middlemen in the process of controlling our economy without direct governmental interference with free individual decision making.

Understanding how and why the banks act as they do in lending and investing is thus basic to a full comprehension of what can and cannot make our economic stabilization policies successful.

It is to this question that we must turn next.

3

The Banker's View of Banking

A commercial bank is a business, and like any other business enterprise, it is out to make a profit. Yet unlike most other businesses, a bank has a deeper obligation than most enterprises to maintain high standards of safety and soundness in its operations, because a bank's operations involve the acceptance and safekeeping of other people's money. For this reason banks are subject to considerable governmental regulation on top of the self-regulation they must exercise to maintain depositor confidence.

To examine what a bank is and does, let us return to the functions of the medieval goldsmith. First of all, the goldsmith had some gold of his own invested in his business. This, in addition to his stature in the community and the possession of an imposing vault, gave the public enough confidence in him to leave their own gold with him and use his receipts for the gold as spending money.

What did the goldsmith actually do? Up till the time he decided to have more certificates outstanding than gold in the vault, he really served as nothing more than a safe deposit vault to those who entrusted their money to him. Once he became a banker through his outstanding certificates exceeding his holdings of gold, his economic function changed. To the individual goldsmith, however, this change in function did not seem great. Before he started to issue certificates in excess of his gold holdings, he felt he had a perfectly valid balance sheet. As assets, he had a certain value of gold. On his liability side, he had outstanding certificates representing this amount of gold. The certificates did not each claim an individual lump of gold; a certificate represented ownership of a certain portion of his total gold holdings. In addition, the goldsmith had his own gold holdings. If he had

not lent these out, his balance sheet would have included more
gold than gold certificates outstanding, with the extra item on the
liability side matching this surplus of gold being labeled something like "capital invested."
His balance sheet would have looked something like this:

Assets		Liabilities	
$120	gold	$110	gold certificates outstanding
		$ 10	capital invested

Because an additional source of income for the goldsmith was
lending out his own gold for interest, his balance sheet would
have changed if a man came in and borrowed some of the goldsmith's own gold. Assuming that the borrower took all the gold
the goldsmith owned, the balance sheet would have looked like
this:

Assets		Liabilities	
$110	gold	$110	gold certificates outstanding
$ 10	loan (note from borrower)	$ 10	capital invested

Very possibly, however, the borrower would not have wanted
gold. He might have preferred to leave with the goldsmith the
gold he had just borrowed and take a goldsmith's certificate instead, because this could be spent as readily as gold and would be
less unwieldy to carry around. In such an event, the goldsmith's
balance sheet would look like this:

Assets		Liabilities	
$120	gold	$120	gold certificates outstanding
$ 10	loan	$ 10	capital invested

To the goldsmith, then, his assets consisted of gold and notes representing borrowers' debts. (The interest the goldsmith earned on his loans may be ignored for the time being. When interest was paid, it was probably paid in gold. This interest increased the goldsmith's gold holdings and the amount represented by "capital invested" on the liability side.)

When the goldsmith decided to have more certificates outstanding than he had gold, it was not a drastic change in his operations. To be sure, up to this point he had always had enough gold to match all his outstanding certificates, but he had also had assets in the form of loans.

When a customer came in to borrow and the goldsmith had no more free gold of his own to lend and decided to lend out gold that was already matched by outstanding certificates, the process was the one he had always followed. The only difference was that the goldsmith was increasing the percentage of loans and reducing the percentage of gold as an asset on his books.

Thus, if the goldsmith's balance sheet had looked like this before:

Assets		Liabilities	
$120	gold	$120	gold certificates outstanding
$ 10	loan	$ 10	capital invested

assuming the borrower took out $5, it would now have looked like this:

Assets		Liabilities	
$115	gold	$120	gold certificates outstanding
$ 15	loan	$ 10	capital invested

If the borrower had decided to leave his newly obtained gold in the goldsmith's vault and to spend a goldsmith's certificate instead, the balance sheet would have looked like this:

Assets		Liabilities	
$120	gold	$125	gold certificates outstanding
$ 15	loan	$ 10	capital invested

To the goldsmith, his operation looked little different from before. All he did was play the law of averages and allow his certificates outstanding to exceed gold holdings, but his actual procedure of accepting gold for interest did not change at all.

Had the goldsmith been told that he was creating money, he would have laughed. "All I do is take in gold and lend out both my own gold and some of the gold left with me by depositors. I'm only lending out part of what I actually have in the vault. I'm not creating money."

The Modern Bank

Turning from the goldsmith to the modern commercial banker, the process is identical.

The individual bank starts with capital funds placed in it by the owners. Before the doors open for the first day of business, the books look like this:

Assets		Liabilities	
$100	cash	$100	capital invested (represented by stock certificates)

After the bank starts business, it receives deposits from customers and makes loans and investments with both its own money and that of its depositors (after arranging to keep enough cash on hand and deposits at the Federal Reserve to meet legal reserve requirements and all but abnormal withdrawals of cash by the bank's depositors).

After the first few days of business, the balance sheet might look like this:

Assets		Liabilities	
$ 60	cash (including legal reserves)	$420	customers' deposits
$340	loans to customers	$100	capital invested
$120	investments in securities		

If the banker were told he has been creating money, he too would say, "You're crazy. All I do is lend out what has been deposited in my bank, plus some of the money that my own stockholders invested when they paid cash to buy their shares of stock. I don't create money."

For the banker this answer is absolutely correct. Although we stated above that the banker creates demand deposits when he makes loans and investments, the actual process is a little more complex.

A banker knows that his deposits remain with him at the pleasure of his depositors and that he must meet withdrawal requests as they occur. Thus he tries to analyze his deposit experience carefully, so as to gauge just what deposit outflow he may expect at any one time.

He knows that his demand deposits come to him in two ways. First, there are the demand deposits he creates when he makes a loan and simply credits his customer's account. These are called *derivative deposits*, in that they are derived from the lending function. Second, he receives deposits when his customers place into their accounts currency or checks written on other people's accounts. Such deposits are called *primary deposits.*

When a banker receives a primary deposit of, say, $100, and his reserve requirement is 20 percent, he has $100 increase in his total reserves of cash and deposits at Federal of which $20 is required reserves to back the new deposit and $80 is excess reserves. From his deposit experience, if he was expecting all this $100 of deposits to leave his bank soon, he would keep $20 in cash or deposit at the Federal Reserve, as required, and he would keep the other $80 either in cash or in very liquid short-term investments, so that when the $100 was withdrawn, he would have enough money to meet the withdrawal.

But his deposit experience is such that generally the banker finds that a primary deposit either stays with him for quite a while, or if it leaves it is replaced by another primary deposit. The volume of currency demanded is fairly stable, and the flow of deposits from bank to bank is also pretty steady. The banker can expect, therefore, that if a check is drawn on this primary deposit and the money moves to another bank, a check written on another bank will be deposited with his institution at about the same time. So the banker keeps the $20 as required reserves and considers that the $80 excess reserves will not be needed to meet deposit withdrawals, and he uses the $80 excess reserves for lending.

If the banker were to lend $400 on the basis of his $80 excess reserve and thereby create $400 of new demand deposits, the transaction would certainly be legal; the $80 of excess reserves would then become $80 of required reserves, and this would be just enough to back the $400 of new demand deposits at a 20-percent reserve requirement. But although it would be legal, it would also be foolish. Unlike the primary deposit, which can be expected to remain with the bank or be replaced as it leaves, the banker has every reason to expect that the $400 of new deposits he creates will not remain with him. The borrower borrowed the money to spend it, and the law of averages shows that this new deposit will not come back to the bank that made the loan; there are about 14,400 other banks at which the recipient of the spent funds can deposit it.

A prudent banker will lend only his excess reserves, in this case $80, because, although he can cover the outflow of $80 by using up his excess reserves, he cannot cover an outflow of $400, assuming he had no excess reserves available before this new primary deposit of $100 was made. To the banker, then, it seems he has done nothing but lend out the $80 extra that he received when the primary deposit was made. He is certain he has not created money.

But what the banker does not see is what happens to the $80 demand deposit created when he makes the loan. He feels that his bank has not created a new deposit, because it soon loses the $80 of deposits he has put on his books, and he loses $80 of reserves along with it. He feels that his deposit creation was only a temporary step, and that all he did was lend $80 of cash and excess reserves at Federal to the person who borrowed money from him. To a banker, as to anyone else, lending cash and money you have on deposit in your bank is certainly not creating new money.

But when the $80 the first banker lends is spent by the borrower and is deposited in a second bank by its recipient, the second bank considers that deposit to be a primary deposit, consisting of money that, on its deposit experience, will remain with it or be replaced if it leaves.

The second bank therefore takes this money, and after setting aside its required reserve and a reasonable additional reserve to handle possible withdrawals, lends the remainder and thereby creates new derivative deposits. The process continues. The borrower of these funds from the second bank spends them, and they are deposited, again as a new primary deposit, in a third bank.

Thus, it must be remembered that while the banking system is creating new money, the individual banker sees only his receipts of deposits and his lending of part of the money he has received. The banker's procedure in operating his bank is similar to the process that a financial intermediary follows. The only major difference is this: The financial intermediary lends money through the physical process of paying out cash or writing a check on its account in a commercial bank; the bank, however, gives the borrower a deposit, a cashier's check, or cash, and as this money is spent by the borrower, the bank also loses either cash or deposits at its own bank, the Federal Reserve.

To be sure, it may come about that a bank makes a loan and creates a new demand deposit, the borrower writes a check on this new deposit, and the check is deposited by its recipient right back in the same bank. In this case, the bank is getting back its own newly created deposit as a primary deposit, and it has actually created money by itself. But it has no way of knowing this. The bank merely accepts deposits from customers. It does not look behind the deposits to see if the depositor got the money from someone who had borrowed it from that same bank. Such knowledge would be meaningless to the banker. Really, all he knows is that a new primary deposit has been made in his bank, and he attempts to lend out the new excess reserves this deposit has brought him if he has not lost an equal-sized deposit at the same time. The operation of the individual banker is clear-cut. He does not feel he is creating money.

In its rudiments, all a bank does is collect funds in the form of capital and deposits and convert this money into assets, in the process trying to earn the maximum profit compatible with the safety of the depositors' funds and the need for liquidity to meet deposit withdrawals.

Most other banking services and operations are directly related to the functions of collection and conversion. Banks handle the transfer of money from account to account as customers write checks. They maintain records indicating the status of each depositor's account. Banks investigate the credit standing of potential borrowers, to determine whom they will lend to, and they then determine what loans to make and what investments to buy.

Banks perform other functions, such as handling estates for individuals and payments to stockholders of corporations in their trust departments, and arranging for international financial transactions. Even these are largely offshoots of the prime function of soliciting deposits and lending and investing the money on hand. The customer's choice as to where he will place his deposit is often influenced by the availability of trust and international services, just as it can be influenced by the location of the bank office, the ease with which a loan can be obtained, and the accuracy with which the bank keeps records of the customers' accounts.

The one feature that makes banking different from any other business is that it accepts depositors' funds and must be ready to pay them back when wanted. Otherwise any manufacturing corporation operates under the same principle as a bank. The manufacturer collects funds from stockholders and from those who become creditors by lending him money or selling him goods and services on credit. He then converts these funds into plant and equipment, raw material, work in process, and inventory of finished goods. The bank similarly collects money from stockholders and creditors, and converts this money into building, loans, and investments. The big difference between banks and manufacturing corporations is that a bank is a place for safekeeping of funds and that customers expect not only that they will get their demand deposits back when they want them but also that the claims on the bank's demand deposits will even serve as money. No creditor of a manufacturing company expects his debt obligation on the company to be as liquid and as safe as the depositor of a bank expects the bank's liabilities to be.

Furthermore, as indicated above, the banks provide the payments mechanism for the whole economy, because about 90 percent of all transactions are settled by check. The government cannot permit the entire mechanism to break down simply on account of banks taking disastrous risks in their effort to maximize profits.

These are the reasons why banks must be so cautious in their operations and why the banking industry must be subject to governmental regulation in addition to that which the Federal Reserve imposes over bank credit creation.

Bank Regulation

Because of the special position of trust that a bank has in the community and the economy, it is subject to more regulation than any other profit-making enterprise. The following are the various forms that this regulation takes.

1. *Regulation on entry.* No one can just open a bank. The request for a charter must be approved by the proper authorities (in the United States this decision is made by either national or state authorities, depending on the type of charter the applicant wants), and these officials are generally hesitant to charter new banks. The reason for the hesitation is that too many banks in a community make all of them unprofitable. This situation leads to riskier loans and investments, because each bank works to maintain profitability. Of course, such risky loans and investments jeopardize the safety of depositors' funds—and it is the safety of deposit accounts that is the prime concern of the supervising authorities.

Even when the regulators feel that a new bank will be a viable unit in the community and will not cause both itself and the existing banks to have to face unhealthy competition, they still require adequate capitalization. This insures that the owners of the new bank have placed enough money of their own into the enterprise to provide an adequate cushion of protection for depositors. If the bank has loans that go bad or otherwise loses money, it is the stockholders' funds that are absorbed first, and the depositors or insuring agency stand to lose only if the losses are in excess of the bank's capital funds.

Finally, after looking at the community's need for the bank and the availability of capital, the regulators ascertain that the proposed bank will have the talent to operate soundly. Only then will a charter be issued. Similar procedures are followed in allowing an established bank to open branches in those states where bank branches are legal.

2. *Regulation of capital.* Not only do bank regulators demand that a bank have a reasonable capitalization before they will issue a charter; but once the bank is in business they also continually check on the relationship between its capital and its deposits and loans to make sure that the cushion of stockholder capital grows as the bank's deposits and risk assets grow.

A bank owner would like to keep his capital position to a minimum, because this provides him with maximum profitability. When a bank makes a profit, it is all channeled into the hands of the bank's owners, that is, the stockholders. If it were possible to have a bank with $1 billion of deposits and only $1 of capital, the holder of that dollar's worth of capital would indeed be a fortunate man, because all the profits earned from lending out the $1 billion of deposit money would be channeled to him.

The more capital a bank has relative to deposits, the more the profits from the deposit solicitation and lending operations are diffused, being shared between a greater number of stockholders, so a bank's owners generally like to keep capital to a minimum for the increased leverage of profit this provides them.

Bank regulators, on the other hand, regard capital as the cushion of money that is available to protect depositors' funds in case of such losses as loan default. Since their aim is to protect the public in its usage of banks, the regulators prefer a bank to maintain a rather high ratio of capital to its outstanding deposits and loans.

The result is a tug-of-war, with the banker generally trying to keep capital low relative to risk assets and the regulators trying to force him to build up his capital either through greater retention of earnings (i.e., paying a lower percentage of earnings out in dividends to stockholders) or by selling new stock as the bank grows.

3. *Regulation over payment on deposits.* Although one would think that the amount a bank pays in interest on deposits would be its own concern, this is not the case. One would expect that no bank would pay out in interest more than it could afford, yet this is not always so. At times competition has forced some banks to pay so much more in interest than they could afford if they bought sound loans and investments that they had to sacrifice asset quality to meet interest demands. To preserve sound banks, lawmakers and regulators have limited the amount that banks can pay in interest. Whereas in other industries unsound practices mainly penalize the owners, in banking, because so large a portion of the available funds is depositors' money, excessive interest payments in effect jeopardize the funds of the depositors who have placed their faith in the bank.

Regulation of interest payments in the United States is of two varieties. First, there is the prohibition of interest payment on *demand* deposits. This was instituted in the 1930s after the failure of a substantial number of American banks before and during the 1933 banking crisis.

It was then thought that one reason for the high incidence of bank failure was the competitive necessity of paying interest on demand deposits. When banks solicit demand deposits, they must provide the depositor with maximum liquidity (this is implied in the fact that the money can be withdrawn on demand), and when banks had to pay interest on these demand deposits as well as absorb the cost of clearing checks and maintaining the records of their customers' accounts, they were also under pressure to make loans and investments that maximized income to cover these high expenses. Many observers feel that the banks, faced with the need for high liquidity and high income, sometimes had no choice but to turn to lower-quality assets as the price of achieving their two goals. The low-quality assets made banks more vulnerable in the Great Depression and thus were one of the factors in bringing on the bank failures of the early 1930s.

Many others feel that this was erroneous thinking. They assert that interest rates the banks were paying on deposits were coming down rather than going up in the 1930s, and that it was other factors—notably an unwillingness of the Federal Reserve to ease credit conditions adequately as economic conditions deteriorated that caused the banking collapse. Thus they hold that the prohibition of interest on demand deposits resulted largely from bankers' efforts to gain legislative aid in their attempts to cut the costs of soliciting deposits rather than from a fear for the solvency of the industry.

In any event this prohibition is slowly breaking down, for several reasons. First, rising interest rates have made solicitation of demand deposits more valuable to commercial banks, and the banks have offered more and more services to depositors to obtain or retain their balances. This practice has reached the point at which many feel it would be less expensive for the banks to start paying interest on checking accounts and charging for the services they now provide free. This has softened the opposition to interest on checking accounts.

More dramatic in its impact was the successful court fight waged by savings bank officials in Massachusetts for NOW accounts. With state-chartered savings banks in that state obtaining the authority to offer accounts providing withdrawal by checklike drafts on interest-bearing savings accounts, the concept quickly spread to all state-chartered institutions throughout New England. Then Congress altered the law to allow federally chartered banks and thrift institutions to offer NOW accounts throughout New England to avoid placing these banks and institutions at a competitive disadvantage against state-chartered banks and thrifts.

It is also likely that in the near future interest on checking accounts through NOW accounts will be allowed nationally. The reason is that credit unions throughout the nation can offer the equivalent of this service by what is called "share draft accounts," which allow credit union members to draw payment drafts on interest-bearing savings accounts. Undoubtedly banks and savings institutions will also be allowed similar powers to avoid a serious loss of a share of the market to the credit union industry.

Moreover banks are developing the practice of transfer of funds by telephone. This practice allows depositors to transfer money between checking and savings accounts by a mere phone call; the next step is likely to be legalization of automatic movement of funds from interest-earning savings accounts into checking accounts as needed to cover outstanding checks. On top of this many banks have developed programs under which the depositor of a savings account instructs the bank by telephone to pay specific bills. Furthermore banks and thrifts are also developing point-of-sale terminals that allow for movement of funds automatically out of savings and checking accounts to pay for goods purchased at a store and automatic deposit to either type of account by giving cash or a check to the grocer or other retailer. All these programs are blurring the differences between savings and checking accounts. And many feel we will soon go the whole way and simply let checking accounts earn interest again.

What about the fear that banks will again have to make risky loans and investments to cover the cost of interest-bearing checking accounts? Most observers hold that these fears are unfounded. As indicated above, some feel that the pressure to make unduly risky loans and investments never developed in the first place. And even those who accept the risky-asset thesis recognize that interest rates are now far higher than when the prohibition was enacted in the Great Depression, so banks can earn enough on quality assets to avoid the need to take undue risks anyway.

Moreover, as we shall see, regulation of bank assets today is stiffer than in the past, which further reduces the fear of banks' taking on too much risk in their loans and investments.

Finally, as is examined immediately below, there are also strict limits on the amount of interest banks can pay on most of the accounts on which they are allowed to pay interest. This also will help prevent the banks from facing earnings squeezes that unfettered interest rate competition might otherwise bring about.

Up to this point, time and savings deposits in commercial banks have not been given much attention, so that the basic distinction could be made between the commercial bank, which can accept and create demand deposits, and the savings bank and savings and loan, which cannot in most states.

As indicated briefly above, however, commercial banks also accept deposits that are not subject to withdrawal by check in the way demand deposits are. And these deposits are now and have always been allowed to offer the depositor an interest payment. Such deposits are divided into two groups: *savings deposits* and *time deposits.* Savings deposits consist of deposits made by individuals on which interest is paid but which can be withdrawn only by presenting a passbook to the bank or by presenting a withdrawal slip to the bank if the account is of the no-passbook variety. This important day-to-day difference between savings deposits and demand deposits is that with the exceptions mentioned above, the withdrawal of funds from a savings account cannot be made by the convenient process of presenting an order on the bank to a third party (i.e., by use of a check). The depositor must be in direct contact with the bank to withdraw his funds. The second difference between a savings account and a demand deposit is that a demand deposit withdrawal must be met on demand for the bank to remain legally solvent; if the bank does not have enough cash available, a savings depositor may be requested to wait for his money for thirty days or whatever waiting time is legally permitted in his particular state.

Although banks seldom take advantage of this delay privilege, it provides them with a safety valve in emergencies. Far more important—because the withdrawal of money from a savings account is much less convenient than writing a check, because many banks do not pay interest on savings accounts unless the money has remained on deposit for a certain length of time, and because the saver does not intend to use his funds to meet day-to-day needs—savings deposits are much less volatile than demand deposits. This lessened volatility, coupled with the fact that in a real once-in-a-lifetime emergency the bank can make the saver wait, enables the bank to be more aggressive in lending out the proceeds of savings deposits than it can be in lending and investing demand deposit funds. This aggressiveness is usually reflected in long-maturity loans and investments, which usually earn higher returns than do shorter-term assets.

The greater stability of savings deposits not only brings greater profitability but also makes the cost of handling and accounting lower than is the case for demand deposits. This makes it possible for banks to pay interest on savings deposits without as much earnings pressure as would be the case if they had to pay interest on demand deposits. Hence, interest on savings deposits has always been legal. But the maximum rate banks can pay on savings is regulated by the banking authorities to avoid cutthroat competition that could hurt the banks.

In addition to savings deposits, banks also accept *time deposits.* These are different from savings deposits principally in that a time deposit is made for a contractually specified time period, and after that time interest ceases to be earned. Unlike the savings deposit, which remains on the bank's books earning its holder interest as long as the depositor wishes, the time deposit matures at a certain, known future date. Because of the stability built into the time deposit and the consequent lessened need for bank liquidity, and because of the low cost of handling a one-shot deposit, banks can pay interest on time deposits and still make a profit on lending and investment of the proceeds without sacrifice of asset quality.

The public use of time deposits serves as an example of how bank deposit solicitation is regulated. Until the mid-1960s, the main users of time deposits were profit-making corporations, since these institutions were then not allowed to hold savings deposits.

The prohibition against corporate holding of savings accounts developed because bank regulators feared that if they were allowed to do so, corporations would remove a considerable portion of their excess funds from their checking accounts and place it in interest-earning savings accounts. A bank has no assurance how long money will be kept in a savings account, but because of the law of averages and because savings account money is not very volatile the bank can generally place savings deposit proceeds into long-term loans and investments without fear of a liquidity squeeze.

If banks were to have savings deposits from corporations, the situation might be quite different. Corporations keep far larger amounts on deposit than individuals, and the removal of even one large corporate savings deposit could cause a serious liquidity problem for the bank losing the funds.

Furthermore, a corporation, with its large balance and numerous employees, would not find the process of actually going to the bank to make a withdrawal anywhere near as onerous as it is for the small saver, and corporations could in effect use savings accounts as the equivalent of interest-bearing checking accounts—moving money out of the savings account and into the checking account only on the day the money was needed, and otherwise receiving interest, if the timing of the deposit matched the bank's interest period requirements.

To avoid what in effect would be interest on demand deposits for corporations, until recently the United States prohibited banks from accepting savings deposits from profit-making corporations. (Schools, churches, and other nonprofit corporations have generally been exempted from this prohibition.) And although the outright prohibition on corporate savings deposits has recently been eliminated, business corporations today are still limited to a maximum of $150,000 in a corporate savings account to avoid the type of deposit outflow and liquidity squeeze that heavier corporate fund flows could cause.

However, a time deposit, on which interest payment is dependent upon the funds remaining on deposit for a contractual period, denies the corporation the possibility of having its money on demand and also gives the bank a far better understanding of its liquidity needs, since it knows when the money must be paid back. Banks are allowed to offer profit-making corporations the time deposit, and this has been a major source of bank deposits.

In late 1964, moreover, the Federal Reserve Board and the Federal Deposit Insurance Corporation instituted a regulation allowing commercial banks to pay more interest on individuals' time deposits than on their savings deposits, again in part because of the greater predictability inherent in the time deposit. In the competition resulting from this ruling, banks started aggressively to solicit time deposits from individuals also; and because they provided a more favorable rate than the banks could offer on savings deposits, time deposits for individuals developed into a popular instrument. At the present time the ceilings on the interest rates that banks and thrift institutions may offer savers has thus become one of the most heated issues in banking.

At this writing, the savings banks and savings and loans are generally allowed to offer a differential of ¼ percent above what commercial banks are allowed to pay on savings deposits and time deposits of under $100,000. The thrifts feel this differential is vital and indeed should be widened if they are to survive against the competitive threat of the commercial banks, with their larger variety of services and far greater number of office locations. Commercial bankers feel, however, that as the thrifts gain more power to use the savings account as a vehicle for bill paying and money transfer, even this present differential should be eliminated. For the time being, the differential is likely to remain because of the violent opposition to its removal from thrift industry forces.

Moreover, many observers, especially among academics, feel that the entire concept of interest rate ceilings on savings is anticonsumerist. These ceilings, most typified by the Federal Reserve's Regulation Q, prevent banks and thrifts from paying the saver more than specific rates on his money even when they can afford to do so and desire to pay the saver more.

Other banks and thrifts feel, however, that removal of these ceilings would bring cutthroat competition and would lead to the demise of many smaller and weaker financial institutions. The prospect here is for maintenance of the ceilings. But they may be raised to a degree for both banks and thrifts, with the ¼ percent differential kept intact.

4. *Regulation of assets.* Finally, the type of assets banks may hold and the interest rate they may charge on loans are regulated. Ownership of certain types of assets is directly prohibited, other types are subject to quality restraints, and there are regulations insuring that liquidity standards are being met and the loan portfolio is diversified.

Most state-chartered banks and all nationally chartered banks are prohibited from owning equity stock (except stock of the Federal Reserve Bank of its district if it is a member bank; stock of subsidiaries of the bank, such as a computer service company; and stock taken over by default when the loan for which it is collateral "turns sour"). Bank ownership of common stock is not prohibited in many other countries; but in the United States it is proscribed. This is due to the feeling that if banks could own stock, they might control much of the American economy through their tremendous financial strength. Bank ownership of equity stock is virtually prohibited to insure that there is a firm separation between ownership of banks and ownership of American business. (Bank trust departments, however, can and do hold stock as trustees for the owners.)

The restraints on bank asset quality are intended to protect the depositor from having his bank fail and lose all or some of his money along with that of the stockholders. Restraints on the quality of loans involve direct examination of banks' loan portfolios by government examiners, to make sure that loan repayment is likely. Banks are forced to write off assets that are considered questionable by the examiners and to subtract from bank capital the amount written off. (If this lowers bank capital below minimum acceptable standards, the bank is told to raise more.)

Banks are also restricted in the percentage of the value of a home they can lend the mortgage borrower, so that if a homeowner fails to make his payments, the bank has not lent more on the home than it can be sold for.

The banking industry is also limited in how much it can lend to one borrower, so that a bank does not have all its eggs in one basket. This limitation usually prohibits the bank from lending any one borrower an amount in excess of 10 percent of the capital and capital surplus that stockholders have placed in the bank and which the bank has earned but not paid in dividends. The purpose of this is to insure that even if a borrower fails, the full loss can easily be covered by stockholders' capital funds, and depositors or the insurers will not suffer any loss.

Banks are limited in their power to make loans to their own officers and directors; the closeness of the relationship between such borrowers and the bank might otherwise take precedence over sound lending standards. Banks are also examined and regulated with regard to the overall liquidity of their lending and investment portfolios, so that they will be able to meet all but the most abnormal deposit withdrawals without having to sell assets in a hurry at distress prices or to impose delays in payment on savings deposit withdrawals.

Finally, banks are limited by usury laws as to how much they can charge an individual (but normally this restraint does not apply on loans to corporations). This last restraint, unlike the others, is intended to protect the borrower. Frequently, however, it merely results in the potential borrower's being denied funds altogether. The lending institutions simply avoid types of loans and states where usury ceilings limit what they can charge, and take their money where they can obtain the going rates for funds. Usury ceilings thus do not bring cheaper money; they frequently bring no money.

The other constraints on bank operations, aside from usury ceilings, have the different purpose of insuring the soundness of the bank and thus the safety of the deposit funds entrusted to it. They generally acheive their purpose far more satisfactorily than do usury ceilings.

As will be seen later, there is also considerable interest today in governmental and regulatory intervention to direct bank funds to uses felt to be of special social interest.

Up to now this so-called approach of *credit allocation* has not been too significant for the industry. And apart from reporting regulations to insure that banks do not *redline* certain areas by refusing to make mortgage loans to anyone in these locations— whether credit-worthy or not—bankers are still pretty much in command of where they lend and to whom, as long as they meet the safety standards established.

These are the basic regulatory constraints—other than re-straints on branching, which will be examined later—within which individual banks operate. Although they and the Federal Reserve's credit controls limit banks' freedom to solicit deposits, manage capital, and use available funds, there is still a vast amount of freedom of decision left to the banking industry.

Where the banks obtain their funds and what choices are avail-able to them in utilizing this money is the next topic that must be examined. Only then can we turn to the key question of how the banks actually allocate the money available to them in the various phases of the business cycle.

4

Sources and Uses of Bank Funds

The best way to approach the problem of analyzing the sources of bank funds and what banks do with the money they receive is to look at the bank balance sheet of assets and liabilities. Exhibit 1 presents the balance sheet for the Schmidlap National Bank and Trust Company as of December 31, 1978.

What should be immediately obvious is that the balance sheet balances. This demonstrates the first principle of banking—and every other corporate enterprise for that matter—that the bank itself owns nothing. Everything the bank has is owned by someone. If the liabilities to depositors and others do not use up the full value of the bank's assets, then the rest belongs to the stockholders and is owed to them.

This can probably be explained a little more clearly in a different manner. Since a bank is nothing more than a corporate name, every asset that the bank has must have been obtained with funds supplied by someone. Thus, the bank's assets are the uses of funds, or things that the bank has placed its money into. Conversely, the liabilities of a bank are the sources of funds, or the explanation of who supplies this money and to whom it really belongs.

This is easy to understand when it applies to deposits and capital, because they are placed in the bank by depositors and stockholders respectively and are then converted by the bank into assets. But even with money earned by a bank's operations, the same principle holds. When a bank makes a profit, the money earned is either placed into new loans and investments or maintained as cash; but no new deposit claims arise to match the asset growth. The liability that increases is the bank's retained earnings or capital position—which is, of course, owed to the stockholders.

The basic sources of bank funds, as discussed above, are its deposits and stockholder investment. As Exhibit 1, the Schmidlap

National Bank balance sheet shows, however, the breakdown of liabilities by category is a little more complex than just deposits and capital. A brief definition of the various liability items follows.

Deposits. This item is, of course, the total of all funds placed into the bank's demand, savings, and time deposits. Most banks do not break down deposits into these three categories in their statements, but the figures are available for internal use and usually for interested parties who desire to know the breakdown.

Deferred income. This account represents the sums collected from borrowers when all the interest due over the life of the loan is deducted from the amount given the borrower at the time the loan is made (this process is called "discounting"). If the bank were to include in earned income its interest on discounted loans before

Exhibit 1 Balance Sheet   Schmidlap National Bank
and Trust Company, December 31, 1978

Assets	
Cash and due from banks	$ 8,299,000
U S. government securities	11,100,000
Municipal and other securities	5,890,000
Federal Reserve Bank stock	185,000
Loans and discounts	59,200,000
Reserve for loan losses	(590,000)
Net loans	$58,610,000
Accrued interest receivable	352,000
Bank building and equipmen	1,940,000
Other assets	282,000
Total resources	$86,658,000
Liabilities	
Deposits	$74,970,000
Deferred income	1,100,000
Operating reserves	614,000
Other liabilities	490,000
Subordinated capital debentures	2,000,000
Capital stock	3,212,000
Surplus	3,960,000
Undivided profits	312,000
Total liabilities	$86,658,000

the customer has had the use of the proceeds for the full time period agreed upon, it would be including in earned income monies it has not really earned yet. Not only would this be dishonest accounting, but it would also force the bank to pay income taxes on the money before it has really been earned. By setting this money aside and considering it still a liability to the borrower, the bank defers income taxes until the time this money truly has been earned.

Operating reserves. The money for operating reserves is set aside in the bank's accounting to meet deposit interest payments and other operating expenses that have been incurred as time passes but which have not yet been paid. The money that will be used to meet these payments is on the asset side of the balance sheet in the form of cash or short-term investments, just as money not yet earned but set down under "deferred income" on the liability side of the balance sheet, is also in the bank in some asset form. But because the money that will go to pay deposit interest or to meet bank expenses is not earned income but money being held until it must be paid out, the bank sets up the operating reserve liability item. This shows that the money has not been earned for the stockholders but belongs to the depositor, the bank's janitor, or to someone else who will receive it soon.

To summarize, the deferred income account is a liability category for money already in the bank but not yet earned, so that the money is not placed into the income account and is not considered as stockholders' earnings too soon. The operating reserve takes cash and other assets soon to be paid out and allocates them to a special liability account; otherwise the only way the bank can balance the balance sheet is to call this money and assets part of stockholder's earned income—which it is not.

One possible confusion must be cleared up at this point. It concerns the term "reserves." Earlier in this book "reserves" was used to describe the reserve requirement a bank must meet to satisfy the Federal Reserve Bank. Now it has been used to describe an accounting category representing money that may have to be paid out soon.

To resolve this confusion it must be pointed out that the reserves the Federal Reserve Bank requires member banks to maintain (and most states require banks that are not members of the

Federal Reserve System to maintain) are asset reserves not even listed on the balance sheet. They are included in the asset item "cash and due from banks," which will be examined shortly. The Federal Reserve simply requires that banks maintain a certain amount of reserves in the form of cash in the bank's vaults or in deposits with the Federal Reserve Bank of its district. Although a certain amount of cash and deposits serves to meet legal requirements of the Federal Reserve and the rest of the cash and Federal Reserve deposit a bank has does not, cash is still cash, and so it is listed as such on the balance sheet.

The reserves that are considered bank liabilities, on the other hand, do exist on the balance sheet. These reserves, however, are bookkeeping items reflecting the fact that money the bank has taken in has not actually been earned or that expenses have been incurred but not yet paid. In order to offset this increase in assets without showing unearned money as having been earned, a reserve category is established to show that the money is in the bank but that it really belongs to certain people or to an emergency fund and is not the property of the stockholders.

Other liabilities. This item, covering liabilities not included elsewhere, mainly consists of some undisbursed loan proceeds held for borrowers, taxes owed, cash dividends due, and other accounts of a temporary nature subject to adjustment.

Subordinated capital debentures. This item is a type of capital recently approved for issuance by banks, which helps to solve the conflict between examiners and bankers over capital adequacy. As will be recalled, banks try to keep capital to a minimum, because selling new stock dilutes the equity and spreads the earnings of the bank over more shareholders. On the other hand, the bank examiners desire capitalization ratios to be maintained at a high level to provide the depositors with a larger cushion of owners' funds for absorbing losses from operations before the depositors themselves are hurt.

The subordinated debenture provides a good compromise; it is an instrument issued when a bank borrows money on the capital market or from other sources, such as its own customers, that will serve as part of its capital cushion. Since the debenture holders receive a claim that is subordinated to the claims of depositors, the debenture proceeds assume a middle position between capital stock and deposits. Thus, when a bank has losses to absorb, the debenture proceeds will not be touched unless all the equity capital has been used up; yet the depositors do not lose a cent until all the debenture funds are utilized to meet the remaining losses. For depositors, then, the debenture provides a satisfactory cushion against loss.

Moreover, because the debenture proceeds are borrowed funds, there is no dilution of equity in the bank and therefore no new stockholders sharing in the bank's profits. All a debenture holder gets is his interest and the return of his principal, and the remaining earnings of the bank still accrue to the same number of shareholders.

The Capital Dilemma

Because of its low cost as capital, the debenture also solves another dilemma for the bankers. Whereas the bank would like to keep capital as low as possible relative to deposits to maximize stockholders' profits, for two reasons it is also influenced by the desire to keep its capital-to-deposits ratio high. First, the larger the capital base, the higher the bank's lending limit to one customer, since the legal lending limit in most states is 10 percent of capital and surplus. Moreover, a bank with a large capital base is less likely to be pressured by the regulators to limit its new lending than would be a bank with a lower capital cushion. Thus a strong capital position serves as a signal to potential customers that this bank will be able to meet loan demands as they develop more easily than a less well capitalized bank could.

Second, a bank with a high capital-to-deposits ratio generally finds its examiners more lenient when they look at the bank portfolio and more willing to allow the bank to hold longer-term, and somewhat lower-quality, assets, which have higher yields. For when the capital cushion protecting the depositors is ample, the risk to the public from an aggressive portfolio is minimized.

Banks, therefore, have a choice between less capital accompanied by greater leverage of earnings (since all available earnings are channeled to fewer stockowners) and more capital accompanied by a more aggressive and profitable loan and investment portfolio.

When all capital was in equity form, for most banks the advantage of leverage more than offset the value of the aggressive portfolio, so they concentrated on keeping capital-to-deposits ratios low. But now, through the use of low-cost debenture capital, banks can "have their cake and eat it too" by increasing capital (so that they can then increase both their deposits and their portfolio aggressiveness) while not dividing earnings among more shares of stock.

To be sure, the debenture is more risky than equity, because the debenture interest must be paid year in and year out, whereas stockholders are paid dividends only when the bank earns them. But the interest paid on debentures is a tax-deductible expense, and the stronger capital position that debentures provide makes the bank a more attractive depository for large corporate balances, which are not protected by FDIC insurance above the first $40,000 on deposit. The debenture has been extremely well received as a compromise between the banker and the examiner in gaining adequate bank capitalization.

Capital stock. Capital stock is the nominal, or par, value of the stock originally bought by the bank's shareholders or purchased later by them when new stock has been sold. It also includes the nominal value of stock distributed to stockholders in stock dividends. There is very little real difference between capital and surplus, because all amounts contributed by stockholders over the nominal value of their stock go immediately into surplus.

Surplus. This item consists of contributions by stockholders above the nominal value of the stock and capitalized undivided profits. Income earned by the bank goes into undivided profits. Then, if the bank feels it wants to retain part of these profits permanently as part of its capital base, instead of paying them out in dividends, it often capitalizes this part of the undivided profits by moving them up into surplus. Since capital stock, surplus, and undivided profits are all the property of the stockholders, this switch from undivided profits to surplus is really merely a bookkeeping item, except that dividends may not be paid from surplus.

Undivided profits. Undivided profits, as indicated above, includes all funds earned by the bank and not allocated elsewhere. This is a liability item, because the new income is actually owed by the bank to its shareholders, even though it has been left in the bank, temporarily or permanently, for the bank's use.

The liability items discussed above comprise virtually all the major sources of bank funds, with the exception of funds borrowed for short periods from the Federal Reserve discount window and the excess reserves of other banks, called *federal funds,* which are frequently borrowed for short periods to meet a bank's reserve deficiency at the Federal Reserve. There are also other sources, such as the funds large city banks may borrow from their overseas branches, called "Eurodollars." Some banks list these items separately; others include them under "other liabilities."

Before discussing how and why the banks allocate these funds into the asset categories that they choose, a brief definition of the various asset groups in the Schmidlap National Bank balance sheet will be worthwhile.

Cash and due-from-banks. This category includes a number of different assets. First, of course, it includes currency and coin kept in the vault and tellers' cages to serve the public.

In addition, the deposit kept by member banks at their district Federal Reserve Bank is included as a "due-from-banks" item. Part of this sum kept at the Federal Reserve is, of course, maintained there to meet the reserves required of member banks. But banks also keep deposits at the Federal Reserve for the same purpose as we keep deposits at our own local commercial bank. We maintain bank deposits so that we can cash checks and draw out currency, and so that when we write checks we have money in the bank to cover them. Similarly, a bank keeps a deposit with Federal so that it can obtain currency when needed for its own operations, and so that when checks written on the bank by the bank's own customers are deposited in another bank and sent to the Federal Reserve Bank for collection, the former bank will have enough on deposit at the Federal Reserve to cover the checks as they are presented for payment by the Federal on behalf of the receiving banks.

Banks that are not members of the Federal Reserve System maintain similar reserves and clearing deposits, but instead of having them at Federal Reserve Banks they maintain them at other commercial banks.[1]

Even member banks of the Federal Reserve System keep demand deposits with other commercial banks to compensate them

[1]The significance of the fact that many banks do not belong to the Federal Reserve System will be discussed later.

for such services rendered as investment advice, trust advice, and especially collection of checks (frequently it is faster or easier for a bank to clear checks directly with other banks than through the Federal Reserve System, even when both banks are members of the system). Banks that keep deposits with other commercial banks are considered to be *correspondents* of one another, and the balances maintained at correspondent banks are a considerable portion of the total cash and due-from-banks item.

Finally, the cash and due-from-banks item includes sums that are not on hand but which will be received from other banks when checks the Schmidlap National has received, drawn on these other banks and now in the process of collection, have been cleared. The bank considers the deposit by its customers of these checks on other banks to be part of the customer's deposit account even though the checks have not been collected yet. (The deposits, however, are considered *uncollected funds* rather than *good funds* until the checks clear and Schmidlap's deposit at Federal has been increased accordingly.) Yet because it has increased its liabilities by the amount of the checks, the bank must offset this item by increasing an asset item, "checks in process of collection," which is also included in the cash and due-from-banks category.

U.S. government securities. This item includes all U.S. government securities held by the bank, no matter how diverse their maturity dates may be. The U.S. government securities category may include bonds that do not come due for twenty years and treasury bills that mature early next week. It is therefore impossible to tell how liquid a bank is from the balance sheet (liquidity being defined as the ability to convert an asset into cash quickly without undue loss), though one can tell how much the bank has in riskless assets. For government securities are felt to be absolute top-quality credits without any long-run risk of loss, if one can hold them to maturity, even though it may at times be difficult to sell long-term governments immediately without sacrifice of value, for reasons that will be discussed later.

Municipal and other securities. This item consists of the obligations of state and local governments, the income of which is exempt from federal income taxes. Because of their tax-exemption feature, banks buy municipal bonds to obtain interest income that is relatively high when compared with the after-tax yield on taxable loans and investments.

Federal Reserve Bank stock. This is the stock in the local district Federal Reserve Bank, which a member bank must buy. The amount a bank must hold is determined by its capital and surplus, and it is not allowed to buy more than it is required to hold. The Federal Reserve pays 6 percent annually in dividends on this stock. As the balance sheet of the Schmidlap National Bank shows, this is a minor item in terms of absorption of bank funds.

Loans and discounts. Loans and discounts should be the largest asset item in a bank. It includes the loans made to the bank's customers, on which interest is paid periodically or at maturity, and the discounts, on which interest is deducted in advance from the money given the borrower.

This item includes loans made by the bank to other banks when these other banks are in need of reserves at Federal or of money for other short-term use. These loans, in the form of temporary transfers of reserves on the books of the Federal Reserve banks, are called federal funds transactions. Loans and discounts also include commercial and industrial loans; loans based on the collateral of stocks, bonds, or other marketable securities; mortgage loans, installment loans, and all other individually negotiated loans to individuals and business borrowers. (It will be remembered that the basic difference between a loan and an investment in a bond is that in investing in a bond the bank provides only part of a large borrowing from many individuals and institutions that is evidenced by a large number of identical loan instruments called bonds, notes, or debentures, whereas a loan is negotiated privately between the borrower and the bank.)

Reserve for loan losses. Because banks have no assurance that all loans will be paid, they set aside a reserve for loan losses. The reserves used to be listed on the liability side of the balance sheet; like other reserves on the liability side, they offset money that is already in the bank and is not owed to depositors but cannot truly be called part of the shareholders' income, since the funds may be lost if loans go "sour."

Recently regulators have determined that this reserve should be placed on the asset side as a "contra asset" or a deduction from loans outstanding, so that readers of the statement can compare loans outstanding with reserves available to meet loan losses.

Because this contra account reduces the asset "loans and discounts," it leads to a reduction in the liability item "undivided profits," so it still reduces shareholder income just as other reserves on the liability side do.

The amount that banks generally carry as a reserve for loan losses is determined by tax laws and by Internal Revenue Service rulings.

This reserve is of great value to banks, since every cent the IRS allows the bank to place into its reserve for bad debts means that much less recorded income and that much less income tax payment. The bank still has the money, invested in cash or other assets, but instead of considering it earned money owed to stockholders, the bank considers it money that *may* be lost because of bad loans, and thus not income. The reserve for loan losses provides additional cushion to protect depositors' funds, but unlike money placed in the undivided profits account, this money is not subject to taxes before it is placed in this category.[2]

[2]Although the general heading "reserve for loan losses" should be adequate for most students of banking, the issue is actually more complex. The amount a bank feels it needs to set aside as a reserve to cover shaky loans, otherwise called the *valuation reserve,* and the amount the IRS permits it to set aside as a deduction from income for tax purposes may be two different amounts.

If the IRS permits the bank to set aside more than the bank feels it needs in its valuation reserve for loan losses, it deducts the extra amount from pretax earnings, just as it deducts the valuation reserve from pretax earnings. But instead of showing the amount as a contra asset against loans, the bank shows it on the liability side.

The amount of the reserve is broken into two parts. The amount of taxes saved by not reporting this additional amount as income is the deferred tax portion and is placed under the "other liabilities" category. It is truly a liability, because eventually the IRS will collect this money from the bank if loan loss reserves exceed actual losses taken.

The rest of this extra amount set aside over and above valuation reserves is really after-tax bank income that has not been reported as such to save taxes. In order to gain the tax benefit the bank has set aside more income to meet loan losses than it actually feels it will need. This is the contingency portion of the reserve and is placed just under "undivided profits"—the proper location, because the amount is really after-tax bank profit that is available as capital cushion like any other after-tax profits. It just has not been reported as such on the earnings statement and balance sheet.

If the bank feels it will need even more of a loan loss reserve than the IRS allows, it must first pay taxes on the additional money and then set the rest aside as a reserve. Handled in this way the reserve is called a *tax-paid contingency reserve* or may be listed as *contingency reserve (tax paid)*; it is also placed just under "undivided profits."

If loan losses actually do exceed what the IRS has allowed as a reserve, the bank then reduces this reserve to cover the losses, after first recapturing the taxes paid. In effect the money is treated just as undivided profits are. But the bank does not wish to call the money profits, because it fears it will lose the money later if the loans it worries about actually do go "sour."

Accrued interest receivable. This item consists of the amount of uncollected interest the bank has earned on loans and investments as of the statement date. If the bank were to consider these sums as income only on the date on which they are actually paid and not accrue them evenly over a period, its income would rise and fall irregularly. Naturally, that portion of interest income which has already been earned but not yet been paid to the bank must be considered an asset on the bank's books. If the assumption were realistic that all this income would be profit and none of it absorbed by operating expenses or losses, this new asset would be matched by a rise in the undivided profits category.

Bank building and equipment. This item describes the present value (after normal depreciation) of the quarters, furniture and fixtures, and equipment used in the conduct of the bank's business.

Other assets. Prepaid expenses and insurance premiums, and items temporarily held in this account pending collection or allocation to other accounts comprise most of the assets included in this final catchall category for assets not specifically mentioned elsewhere.

These, then, are the categories in which banks' fund sources and uses can be placed. Once they are understood, the key problem of banking must be faced: How shall we allocate our available funds among the various asset categories and borrowing customers of the bank.

5

The Allocation of Bank Assets

Although commercial banks have some control over both their assets and their liabilities, the choice available to the banker is far greater in controlling assets than in managing liabilities.

A bank can determine how much capital it wants to start with, and whether it will sell new stock to obtain additional capital as the bank grows, or build capital solely by retaining more earnings and paying out less to the stockholders in dividends. It also has some control over the increase in its deposits. It can attract new checking accounts by lowering the charges to customers for handling their checks, and it can increase its time and savings deposit accounts by offering more attractive interest rates, though always below or at the ceilings established by the regulators.

Although these efforts have some impact on bank liabilities, most banks, especially those in small communities, find that increases in their deposits are dependent mainly upon the wealth of their locality and the competition they face there from other institutions. Thus, with the exception of a few large banks that are able to attract money from all over the nation, and of those banks, both large and small, which are willing to encourage growth by paying well above going rates for time and savings funds when allowed by the regulators, most banks consider their liabilities to be more or less determined for them. They concentrate their efforts on asset management or on the allocation among the various asset categories of the funds available.

Whereas the choice available to the bank in asset allocation appears wide, a bank must follow several basic rules in converting into assets funds obtained on the liability side. These rules lessen the banker's choice to a considerable degree.

First, a banker must place some of his available funds into building and equipment before he can even start his bank. A bank must also maintain satisfactory levels of *primary* and *secondary* *reserves*.

Primary reserves are of two basic forms: cash needed to operate the bank, and cash and deposits at the Federal Reserve (or at correspondent banks for nonmembers of the Federal Reserve System) that must be maintained to meet the bank's reserve requirements. These are both essential to the functioning of a bank; without vault cash, a bank cannot open its doors and serve the customers, and without meeting its legal reserve requirements a bank cannot lawfully remain open.

As has been seen, primary reserves are all part of the cash and due-from-banks category in the balance sheet; but this cash and due-from-banks item also includes other money maintained in this liquid form, available in case of an adverse flow of funds from the bank.

What should be recognized is that bank primary reserves are not really reserve money at all in the way we as individuals consider reserves. We look at our own reserves as money available for emergencies. A bank cannot treat its primary reserves in this way. In an emergency, when depositors want their money back unexpectedly, the one asset category that cannot be utilized to meet these payments is the bank's required reserves.

To be specific, if a bank is fully loaned up (i.e., if it has just enough in cash and deposits at Federal to meet its legal reserve requirements) and customers unexpectedly withdraw $1 million, the bank cannot use its primary reserves to meet this fund outflow, because then it will not have enough primary reserves left to back all its remaining deposits. It is true that when $1 million leaves the bank, the $200,000 of primary reserves that served as required reserve backing for this $1 million of deposits is freed (assuming a 20-percent reserve requirement) and can serve to help cover the fund outflow. But the remaining $800,000 must be found elsewhere; the rest of the bank's primary reserves must be kept to back remaining deposits.

Instead of serving as a reserve for contingencies, the primary reserve that a bank must maintain is really not available for emergency use at all (except for the fractional backing of the deposit that actually leaves the bank). Rather, its function is to make credit control policy work. Instead of serving as the source of liquidity that a reserve in the true sense is, a bank's primary reserve is one of its least liquid assets.

For this reason banks maintain, in addition to their primary reserves, a secondary reserve of money kept in fairly liquid form that can be utilized to cover deposit outflows and to meet unexpected loan demands.

The secondary reserve, unlike the primary reserve, can be maintained in earning assets. Cash does not earn any return, and the money that banks must maintain as required reserves with either Federal Reserve or with correspondent banks must be held in demand deposit form, and demand deposits cannot legally earn interest either (although in several states banks that are not members of the Federal Reserve System may keep part of their primary reserves in certain securities that pay interest). After banks have satisfied their required primary reserves, then, they take a certain portion of their deposit funds and place it into assets that are extremely liquid, although not as liquid as cash or demand deposits, which also yield a return.

There is no category labeled secondary reserves on the bank balance sheet, because secondary reserves may be in the form of investments in short-maturity U.S. government securities, loans to brokers and dealers in securities, purchases of short-term commercial paper (which are IOUs issued by commercial corporations), and short-term investments issued by state and local governmental units.

The characteristic feature of the loans and investments in secondary reserves is their liquidity; they can be converted into cash quickly without undue loss of principal. Generally this situation is achieved by holding only very short-term loans and investments in the secondary reserve, since these can always be redeemed at par value when they mature and the maturity dates are never far away on short-term assets.

How much a bank must keep in its secondary reserves depends upon the deposit experience of the bank, the volatility of its liabilities, and the requirements of its examiners. Deposit experience plays an extremely important role here; the bank wants to be sure that it can meet all but the most serious fund outflows without undue reliance on the Federal Reserve's discount facilities. Although the Federal Reserve discount window is available to help banks meet the type of deposit outflows that secondary reserves guard against, it must be remembered that as a private enterprise a bank desires to manage its day-to-day operations with minimal reliance on help from the central bank.

Once a bank has provided funds for its building and equipment, for its Federal Reserve Bank stock, and for its primary and secondary reserves, the remaining funds are free for placement either in loans or in investments. But even here, there is some constraint on the choice available to the banker, since in most aggressively run commercial banks there is no question but that every reasonable request for a loan from a customer should be met if it is humanly possible.

A bank is in the business of lending money. When it makes a loan, it makes a friend of the customer and undoubtedly makes more certain the prospect that the customer will leave his deposit account with it. When a bank makes a loan to an individual or business in its community, it is helping the community prosper and grow, and this prosperity and growth cannot but help the bank prosper too.

Moreover, banks generally earn more on a loan than on an investment—for several reasons. It is to be expected that the rate of interest charged an individual borrower will be higher than that which a bank earns on a bond, because not only does the bank have all the difficulty of arranging the loan transaction, evaluating the credit standing of the borrower, and collecting the interest, but also the individual borrower will most likely not be as creditworthy as a company large enough to sell a bond issue. The bank must be compensated for the higher risk involved as well as the greater expense of making the loan.

As a result, the personal loan repaid in installments is the highest-yielding loan on a bank's books.

On the surface it may look as if an installment loan is relatively inexpensive; it may be advertised as costing only $4 for each $100 of the amount of the loan. Although on the surface the cost of the plan seems to be at the 4-percent rate, a deeper examination will show that the rate is closer to 8 percent. First of all, the loan may be discounted, meaning that the $4 interest is deducted in advance, and so instead of lending the borrower $100 for $4 interest, the bank is really lending him only $96 for the $4 return. This by itself brings the interest rate up to only 4.167 percent, and that is the interest rate charged if the borrower were to keep the bank's $96 for a full year. But he does not. He has the full $96 for one month only, after which he has to pay back one-twelfth of the total due. Each month until the end of a year, at which time he has paid off the bank completely, he pays back one-twelfth more. Thus, instead of keeping the bank's $96 for a year, on average the borrower has really kept about half that much money for a year. He has $96 of the bank's money in the first month, but the amount he holds declines steadily to only $8 in the final month. Thus the true interest is approximately double the 4.167 percent.

It is obvious then that a bank prefers to make as many installment loans as it possibly can. This should explain the paradox of aggressive bank efforts to obtain new installment borrowers at times when the Federal Reserve has made credit extremely tight and the bank is discouraging all other borrowing. One can readily see why banks try to allocate to their installment loan officers all the money they require provided sufficient funds are reserved to meet the borrowing needs of other good customers.

Although bank installment loans provide more return to the bank than appears on the surface, bank business loans also yield the bank more than the stated interest rate when they are handled properly by the bank. Banks require that business borrowers maintain *compensating balances* on deposit commensurate with the size of the outstanding loan. In making a commercial loan, the banker will have it understood by the borrower that he must maintain 15 to 20 percent of the amount borrowed as a demand deposit balance in the bank.

The equity of such a requirement can be questioned. No store requires buyers of goods to leave 15 or 20 percent of their purchases on the shelf after they have paid for them. However, though some people question the whole concept of compensating balances, bankers justify them this way: "If the potential borrower is financially strong enough to borrow money, he is also strong enough to have a bank account. And if he is coming to borrow from me, then it is only right that I should hold his bank account.

Since most firms need a working balance of about one-fifth to one-sixth of their outstanding loans to cover normal operating expenses and contingencies, this is the balance that I will demand."

This balance provides no profit to the bank if the customer utilizes the balance so actively that the work of servicing the customer's checks and handling his other financial requirements more than eats up the profit the bank can earn by lending out the money maintained in the compensating account. But when a compensating balance is kept relatively inactive, it increases the income the bank earns on its business loans to one-fifth or one-sixth above the interest rate actually charged.

Finally, as for mortgage loans, the aggressive bank feels such loans also bring in borrowers' deposits and help serve the community's growth when lent to local people. Banks give local mortgages preference over investments, but out-of-town mortgages, such as those bought through mortgage bankers, are not given preference and are treated more like investments.

There are many reasons, then, why a bank prefers to lend out all it has, over and above the amount that must be tied up in plant and equipment and primary and secondary reserves. The investments of an aggressive bank, other than the investment part of secondary reserves, are truly considered a residual account, receiving funds only when loan demands are not strong enough to use up all the money not tied up in reserves. Whenever loan demands start to pick up, investment officers are usually forced to sell their investments and return the funds to the lending officers.

There is an old story that whenever everyone else is through with the grapes a certain wine company buys them. This can also apply to the investment officer. Only when nobody else has use for money does he get it.

However, the very fact that bank funds are placed into the investment account only when there is no other use for the money makes the commercial bank into a flexible vehicle for the transmission of credit tightness and ease to the economy at large. The investment function is the kingpin of the commercial bank's adjustment to tight and easy money, even though the main impact on the economy is felt through the bank's lending operations.

The Bank in Credit Ease

To understand the basic role of the investment officer in making monetary policy effective, let us assume that the economy is operating well below capacity and that the Federal Reserve is anxious to encourage maximum borrowing and spending to help pull the nation out of the recession. Its basic action will be, of course, to make credit conditions easy by open-market operations, and possibly even by lowering reserve requirements if the situation is serious enough.

Easy money means that the banks are provided free excess reserves. This availability of reserves comes about either through a lowering of reserve requirements or through the Federal Reserve's purchase of securities in the open market, payment being made by giving the banks new deposits at Federal whether they sell the securities or their customers sell the securities and deposit the proceeds. No bank worth its salt wants to sit around with unused excess reserve funds on its hands; each day this money earns no interest means income lost, never to be regained, just as the potential revenue lost by a commercial airplane when it flies with an empty seat can never be recouped. Banks become aggressive in their lending operations when money becomes easy.

The actions banks undertake in such circumstances are of three kinds: lowering borrowing rates, increasing aggressiveness in seeking out loans, and easing of quality and maturity standards in the loans that are placed on the books.

Of course, one would expect banks to lower borrowing interest rates to encourage new borrowing when credit is readily available, just as a store lowers prices when it has too much inventory of an item. Interest rates merely reflect supply of and demand for borrowed funds, just as supply and demand set most other prices. In a period of credit ease the supply of bank funds is increased, because Federal Reserve action has increased the quantity of bank reserves available while the demand for bank credit is fairly weak (a recession reflects the fact that people are less anxious to borrow and spend). Thus interest rates fall. It must be remembered that the Federal Reserve does not lower interest rates itself. All it does is increase the availability of bank reserves. It is the competition among banks and between banks and other lenders to put their new reserves to work in a free-market economy that brings about the decline in interest rates.

Lower interest rates, however, are not by themselves enough to do the full job of encouraging more borrowing in the economy. If a company finds that it has far more inventory than it can possibly sell in the foreseeable future, no decline in the cost of borrowing money is going to spur it to increase its inventory. Similarly, capital expenditure plans are undertaken by companies when manufacturers feel new facilities are needed and will earn a decent return, say, 15 to 20 percent a year or more. In such a setting, there is not much that a decline in the price of bank loans of, say, 1 percent can do to encourage new capital construction. Certainly a decline in interest rate will serve as little encouragement to build new capital facilities when the management of a company feels there is no real market available for the products the new plant would make; and if a project is so marginal that a decline of 1 percent in interest cost (of which about half is a tax deduction anyway) makes a project look feasible when previously it was not, then undoubtedly it should not be constructed in any case.

Thus, the decline in the interest rate is unlikely to encourage much new business spending, although it does shift borrowers back and forth between borrowing from banks and borrowing in the open market. A decline in interest rates is also unlikely to be very important in encouraging new installment borrowing. Installment borrowers generally look at the terms—how much they pay a month—rather than the effective rate of interest. Moreover, installment loan rates being at a high level, a small decrease in the borrowing cost will not be a very significant factor in encouraging new borrowing, even among interest-rate-sensitive borrowers.

It is true that mortgage borrowing can be encouraged to a degree by lowering interest rates, and some marginal impact on business and installment borrowing develops when rates are reduced, but basically banks encourage more lending at times of easy money through increased aggressiveness in lending terms and lending promotion.

Lending terms can be eased in periods of easy money in two ways. First, the amount of time the borrower is allowed to keep the money can be increased; and second, the quality of collateral and/or credit standing demanded of potential borrowers can be lowered to attract new borrowers. These moves can encourage some expansion in bank lending and can also make bank borrowing more attractive than alternative fund sources.

Finally, banks promote lending aggressively in periods of easy money. New techniques are developed, such as "dial-a-loan" service, which allows a potential borrower to make his first contact with the bank by calling a phone number that is serviced twenty-four hours a day, seven days a week. It is in periods of easy money that banks have developed and inaugurated most of their more aggressive lending techniques, such as buying equipment and leasing it to a customer instead of merely making a loan that the customer uses to buy his equipment, and factoring—buying a customer's accounts receivables directly from him for cash without recourse if they are not paid—instead of just lending on the receivables. These are the ways in which banks try to encourage more borrowing and spending when credit is easy. Since the Federal Reserve makes credit easy so as to encourage just such an increase in borrowing and spending in a slack economy, the banks' aggressive boosting of lending in periods of easy money fits right into the posture of bank activity the Federal Reserve hopes to achieve at such times.

The Investment Officer

Even if banks reduce lending rates and become more aggressive in lending terms and more imaginative in lending forms in a period of credit ease, this is not likely to provide the bank with an outlet for all the funds it has to invest. The very fact that the nation is in a recession means that borrowing and spending plans do not match the capacity of the nation to produce goods and services. Thus, whereas some individual banks may have heavy loan demands, the banking system as a whole undoubtedly will not be able to place all of its available funds into loans.

This is when the banks turn to their investment officers and tell them to place the excess funds into investments.

The investment officer does not have an easy job; he knows that at the same time he is trying to find new investment outlets, a great many other commercial banks are looking to the organized capital market as a place for investment of surplus funds.

There is a basic principle in finance: When interest rates rise, bond prices fall. When interest rates fall, bond prices rise. This can be proved by the dilemma that the investment officer faces in a period of easy money.

A *bond* is a promise to repay principal at a certain date and to pay interest annually or semiannually at a rate specified at the time the bond is sold. If the borrower finds that at the time of the original sale the only way he can obtain a market for his securities is to offer 4 percent, he sells his bond with a *coupon rate* of 4 percent, meaning that he will pay the holder of the bond 4 percent ($40 on a $1000 bond) every year until the bond matures. This becomes a fixed obligation, and whether interest rates in general rise or fall, the borrower still is obligated to pay a full $40 a year on each $1000 bond outstanding, no more and no less.

However, if interest rates fall to 3 percent, owing to excess of supply of money over demand, the 4 percent a year that the $40 interest on the $1000 bond represents becomes a high and attractive yield to potential purchasers of bonds. The initial buyer of the bond, who bought it at the time when 4 percent was the going return, now knows that this bond yields more than any brand-new securities available. If he wants to sell it, he can raise the price he charges, until the price becomes so high that the $40 interest earned each year is only a 3-percent return on a new buyer's investment. (If this bond were to remain outstanding in perpetuity, a price of $1333.33 would be necessary to provide a 3-percent yield; but since the new buyer of the bond suffers a capital loss of the difference between his purchase price and the $1000 the issuer will repay at maturity, the price will rise by an amount smaller than $333.33 to make the effective yield to maturity drop to 3 percent. The actual figures are worked out in books of bond yield tables.) The principle should be clear: As interest rates fall, the prices on outstanding bonds rise, so that even though their coupon return, the amount the borrower pays in interest each year, is fixed, the actual *yield* on his investment to the new buyer falls to match current interest rate levels.

Thus, our investment officer is given money to invest in a period of recession, when interest rates are low and bond prices are high. He has a choice between seeking the maximum return he can possibly earn on this investment money and keeping the money in fairly liquid investments. His decision will, of course, be made on the basis of which he thinks will maximize his bank's profit, but, as will be seen, his choice of which investments to buy in a period of recession when money is easy will have a considerable impact on the boosting effect that easy money gives to the economy.

In determining how to invest the money that has been turned over to him, the investment officer must be guided by the *yield curve* for investments then in force. A yield curve is a picture of what bonds of identical quality but differing maturity dates offer as a yield at that moment. A yield curve is presented in Figure 3. The vertical axis shows a scale of yields; the horizontal axis presents the time to maturity of outstanding securities.

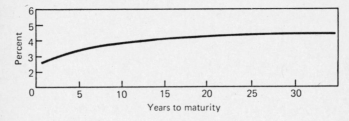

Figure 3   Yield Curve for U.S. Government Securities

A yield curve is called an *indifference curve,* because it shows that lenders and investors are indifferent to the various combinations of yield and maturity available at that moment and consider them equal in value. If they became unsatisfied with one or some of the yield-maturity combinations available, they would sell the securities they did not like and buy more of those whose yield-maturity combination they preferred. This would change the yield curve, since the investors' purchases and sales of securities would alter the prices, and therefore yields, of the issues thus affected.

The very fact that the yield curve does not move indicates that for the time being investors are satisfied with this range of yield levels.

What determines the yields on individual securities, and so the slope of the yield curve, is obviously the supply of and demand for bonds of various maturities. It is possible, however, to go beyond supply and demand and determine to a degree what sets supply and demand.

The determination of supply of and demand for bonds and other fixed-income securities of various maturities is in part set by institutional restraints on time periods for borrowing and lending, which are imposed on the borrowers and lenders in the organized money and capital markets. For example, a company has money to meet a dividend payment in six months and in the meantime wants to place it in the money market. It is not in a position to be flexible in the matter of maturity, because the money must be paid out in dividends six months from the date of the purchase. This is one way in which funds in the money market are restricted in maturity. Similarly, the U.S. government is prevented by law from borrowing over $17 billion at an interest rate of over 4.25 percent, unless the borrowing is for less than ten years. The law is intended to avoid the Treasury's being saddled with high interest rates on its borrowings for long periods, so it prevents the Treasury from utilizing securities of over ten years' maturity at times when interest rates in the open market on U.S. Treasury issues exceed 4.25 percent. Since the Treasury must borrow money when there is a deficit, the restraint on long-term borrowing forces the Treasury to increase its intermediate-term borrowing (of under ten years). This raises the interest-rate level for securities of under ten years on the yield curve and lowers it for those over ten years, since the restraint on the types of securities the Treasury can sell increases the demand for funds in the under-ten-year sector and decreases it in the over-ten-year sector. This brings about a humped yield curve at times, as illustrated in Figure 4.

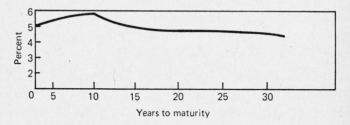

Figure 4 Humped Yield Curve for U.S. Government Securities

The supply of and demand for bonds of various maturities (which, of course, determine the slope of the yield curve) are also affected by the expectations borrowers and lenders in the money and capital markets have of the trend in future interest rates.

If prospective lenders feel that interest rates are going to rise (undoubtedly as a result of their feeling that the economy's growth will increase demand for funds relative to the new supplies that the Federal Reserve will make available and the available savings of the public), they will be unwilling to make loans for long periods at current yields. Obviously if their expectations turn out to be correct, they will be able to get much higher yields on their money by waiting a little while, and also, since as interest rates rise, bond prices fall, confirmation of their expectation of rising interest rates will bring capital losses on securities purchased currently.

At such a time, the only way holders of investible funds can be induced to place their money in long-term investments is to attract such long-term placement by offering considerably higher interest rates on long-term investments than they can obtain on shorter-term ones. Otherwise they will find it worthwhile to buy short-term investments and, as these mature, to place the money into longer-term investments at the higher interest rates expected to be in effect. Thus, the expectation of rising interest rates brings with it an upward-sloping yield curve.

Conversely, if interest rates are expected to fall, there is likely to be a downward-sloping yield curve. Potential buyers of bonds will feel that if they wait too long to make long-term investments, they will have to accept lower returns than are available currently and miss the price increases that come as yields fall. They try to "lock up" their money on long-term investments at current yields, and with many investment officers all bidding for long-term investments to beat yield declines, this pushes up the prices that investors must pay for long-term bonds and thus reduces their yield below that available on shorter-term securities (Figure 5).

The investment officer faces a dilemma. He is given the bank's surplus funds at times when loan demands are fairly weak, and he knows that he will be asked to give this money back to the lending officers when loan demands pick up, because for reasons

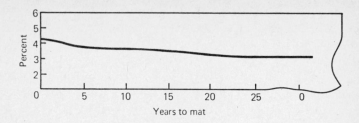

Figure 5   Downward-sloping Yield Curve
for U.S. Government Securities

given above the bank is dedicated primarily to lending to its own customers rather than to investing in the impersonal bond mar ket.

But what does the investment officer do with the money while he has it? Regardless of the slope of the yield curve, he has a problem. If the yield curve is upward sloping, this is the difficulty: He can maintain the liquidity of his investment position by keeping the money in short-term securities, so that if loan demands pick up he can redeem his fixed-income securities quickly and without undue loss, and return the money to the loan department.[1] On the other hand, while maintaining liquidity, the investment officer is sacrificing profits, because the yield curve is so constituted that higher returns involve going out into long-term securities. Thus, he can maintain the bank's liquidity, but only at the expense of its profitability.

The other choice available to him is also hard. If he moves into the long-term bond market, he obtains higher yields for the bank. But what happens to him when the economy recovers and loan demands pick up again? As the economy picks up steam and loan demands grow again, the Federal Reserve becomes more conservative in allowing growth in bank reserves, so that the boom does not get out of hand and become inflationary. Under such circumstances, interest rates are bound to rise—owing to the reduced

---

[1] As will be explained later, as interest rates rise, the prices of short-term securites fall less than do the prices of longer-term issues. Thus, if the investment officer wants his money back even before the short-term securities mature, the loss he must accept on selling them when interest rates are rising is well below what he would lose if he were trying to liquidate longer-term obligations.

availability of funds and the increased demands for them—and bond prices consequently start to fall. The investment officer finds himself forced to recapture the money he has placed into bonds so as to turn it over to the loan department to meet rising loan demands. But he is faced with capital losses in selling bonds, because bond prices have fallen since he was given the money to invest.

Because he is a residual user of funds, and therefore gets funds to invest only when bond prices are high, and must return the money as bond prices fall, the investment officer is in the awkward position of taking losses on his portfolio every time there is an economic recovery. His only alternative is sacrificing income during recessionary periods, when banks usually need income badly because lending rates and volume have fallen. The investment officer's job in an economy with a rising yield curve is no picnic. He is damned whether he keeps the money short or places it out long—the only difference is in the reason.

When the yield curve is downward sloping, it looks on the surface as if the investment officer has the best of both worlds. He can maximize liquidity by staying short, and still produce a higher return for the bank than it would gain by placing the investible funds into long-term bonds—at least for the moment.

But there is a hitch in such reasoning. Bearing in mind investors' natural inclination to keep their money liquid when possible (because when the date for return of the principal is early there is greater safety and assurance of repayment), one must ask why lenders should be willing to accept a lower yield for long-term investment than for shorter-term bonds. The reason is again expectation. As will be recalled, the reason for a downward-sloping yield curve is that the capital market expects interest rates to fall. For this reason investors generally will take a lower return for long-term investment than for short-term securities; at least they have the assurance that they will earn this return for a considerable period in the future. If they bought short-term securities, they might soon be faced with the return of their money and have to reinvest it at a time when the yields available on investments of all terms probably will be much lower than those currently available.

Thus the investment officer faces a dilemma even when there is a downward-sloping yield curve. It is true that he can maximize liquidity by staying short and can still get a higher return than he can get by moving into longer-term bonds; yet there is a risk that his high return will be only temporary. When his present short-term securities mature, if interest rates do fall he may look back sadly to the earlier opportunities for long-term, high-rate investment, knowing that if only he had been willing to move into longer-term securities at an earlier date he could be earning higher yields, and earning them for a long time hence.

Faced with a downward-sloping yield curve, the investment officer can either sacrifice potentially greater future profits for the sake of liquidity or get longer investments that should yield more in the near future than short-term securities will. This latter course, however, involves sacrificing the bank's liquidity and the risk of capital losses if capital market expectations should be wrong and interest rates on loans should begin to rise.

The investment officer's dilemma is real, and, as will be seen shortly, the choice the officer will make between long- and short-term investment at any particular time is hard to predict.

His decision will depend on which approach he feels is in the best interest of the bank's overall profitability over a period; yet his choice will have great influence on whether the bank plays a part in spurring economic recovery or whether it remains fairly insignificant as a force in the economy's climb upward from the slump.

The Economic Impact

To the investment officer the choice is simply between short- and long-term securities; to the economy his choice means far more than that. When the investment officer chooses to hold short-term securities, he places his money in short-term U.S. government securites, short-maturity state and municipal borrowings, and other issues that provide the borrower with a source of short-term funds. The impact of this new investment in short-term obligations is to lower money-market interest rates, which facilitates short-term borrowing. Short-term securities reflect only temporary credit accommodation, however; they do not have any major impact on the nation's level of economic activity.

When a bank with weak local loan demand places its funds in long-term bonds of corporations and state and local governments, and in long-term mortgages bought from such out-of-town originators as mortgage bankers, the economic impact is quite different. The utilizers of long-term credits are home builders and home buyers, companies that want to build new plants, and state and local governmental units that want to build new schools, bridges, roads, hospitals, and other public works. It is true that business borrowing is not much affected by the decline in the interest rates that develops as the banks buy more bonds, because as indicated earlier, business borrowing is not very sensitive to interest rate, and lower interest rates by themselves would not encourage much new borrowing. As far as mortgage borrowing and state and municipal borrowing are concerned, however, the decline in interest rates that develops when bank investment officers move out into long-term securities inspires increased borrowing and spending. When planning capital facilities, these groups are far more sensitive to the interest rate than are business borrowers.

Thus, when banks keep their investment funds in short maturities, they play a virtually neutral role in helping the economy recover, other than adding liquidity to the economy. But when they move out aggressively into longer-term investments and purchase more mortgages than they originate themselves, this is a major force in helping the economy to grow back upward from its slump.

The impact of bank purchases of short- and long-term securities respectively is not completely clear-cut, though, because there is a spillover effect in the money and capital markets.

If interest rates drop in the short-term end of the market owing to purchases of securities by banks, this decline immediately makes other borrowers sell shorter securities than they had originally planned to sell, in order to take advantage of the lower borrowing costs in that maturity range. Other lenders move out of short securities to longer ones, because yields on short-term securities have dropped and yields in somewhat longer-term issues have not.

This process of borrowers moving to the short-term end of the market and lenders leaving it increases demands in the short-term maturity range and reduces supply of funds, which leads to a return to somewhat higher interest rates there. However, the reverse develops in intermediate-term securities, and interest rates fall, because borrowers have moved out of this range and new lenders have entered it, lowering interest rates here as they are rising at the short-term end. Bit by bit—like a stack of dominoes falling—the low interest rates that started at the short-term end of the market are transmitted to longer- and longer-term securities, until the entire yield spectrum feels some impact from the short-term security purchases the banks have undertaken.

The spillover effect is not completely effective, because many borrowers and lenders will not or cannot change maturity ranges to take advantage of higher returns or lower borrowing costs. For example, a company with money it will need in six weeks to pay taxes cannot invest that money in twelve-week securities and take advantage of higher yields available there without facing difficulties on tax payment day.

The bank investment officer's decision whether to move into the long end or the short end of the market is thus of major significance to the economy, even though the normal spillover action of the marketplace can moderate its impact to a degree. The Federal Reserve, too, can modify the impact of the bank's decision through its choice of dealing in long-term or short-term securities in its open-market operations.

There is no exact answer to what makes bankers decide to keep investments short at some times and to push them long at others, but some guidelines can be drawn.

Of course, the main consideration that determines whether the bank investment officer is going to place his funds out long or maintain them in shorter-term investments is his outlook for the economy. If he feels that the current recession will be a short one, he will try to keep his position liquid, so that no major capital losses will have to be taken shortly when he reduces his investment holdings and returns the money to the lending officers. Conversely, if he feels that the economy will continue in a slump for a considerable period, he will become more aggressive and place the money into longer-term investments. Obviously, predictions about the movement of the economy are at best educated guesses, and since the banks' economic and interest rate forecasts contain a considerable element of uncertainty, other factors enter into the decision-making process.

One factor is the bank's recent experience in the investment markets. For example, in late 1957 and in 1958 the economy was in a recession. Investment officers were given funds to invest, and much of the money was placed in intermediate- and long-term securities, in the expectation that loan demands would not pick up for quite a while. Also, at that time the yield curve not only was upward sloping but also extremely steep in its slope, because the Federal Reserve was under no international constraint to keep short-term interest rates up when domestic needs were for easy money.

By this is meant that until late 1958 the U.S. dollar was virtually the only convertible currency available for international investment. People could place money for investment into a lot of other currencies, but there was no certainty that they would be allowed to remove their money when they wanted it, because at that time other nations were having difficulties with their international balances of payments, and to deal with the problem they had resorted to strict controls over the removal of money from the country. The U.S. monetary authorities had no reason to worry about international interest rate levels, because for all intents and purposes international investors had no choice but to keep their money here if they wanted to get it back when they desired it. Thus, in 1958 the yield on U.S. Treasury bills—the 90-day investment securities issued by the Treasury—dropped to as little as 0.56 percent.

Faced with a yield curve that sloped sharply upward from 0.56 percent and expecting a long period of weak loan demands, the banks naturally moved money into longer-term investments to take advantage of the higher yields available thereby. Yet economic activity turned around rapidly, and interest rates started to rise quickly, trapping many a bank with intermediate- and long-term securities that were rapidly declining in price and on which serious capital losses had to be taken as the banks converted investment funds to cash in order to meet rising loan demands.

In 1960, when the next period of easy money developed and

bank investment officers were presented again with large quantities of funds to invest, they remembered 1958. They had been badly burned, and as a result they stuck largely to shorter-term investments so that they would not be caught in the sort of liquidity pinch they had experienced in 1958.

Moreover, by 1960 the international financial structure had changed. Whereas in 1958 the Federal Reserve had been able to let short-term interest rates fall as low as the market would take them without worrying about the impact on international fund flows, in 1960 this was no longer the case. In late 1958 the major Western European nations restored full convertibility on current account to their currencies for nonresidents of each respective nation. This meant that foreign investors had many other safe choices than merely holding their short-term investments in dollars. Since international investors could now move their money from dollars into a number of other strong currencies, the United States had no choice but to make short-term interest rates attractive relative to yields available abroad. Otherwise, investment funds would have left the dollar and moved abroad, bringing about an even larger outflow of gold than we were experiencing at that time from other causes. The lowest point to which the Treasury bill yield was allowed to drop in 1960 was 2.2 percent, almost four times higher than the minimum-yield level reached two years earlier.

In 1960 American bank investment officers faced the job of investing their funds with two reasons for preferring to keep money in short-term investments. First, they had been burned in 1958 and they worried about liquidity more than otherwise would have been the case; second, because interest rates on short-term securities were now four times higher than two years earlier, the banks would suffer less of a yield sacrifice if they wanted to remain in short-term investments and not move out long.

In 1960 and 1961 banks kept their investment portfolios short, and they generated little downward pressure on long-term interest rates on tax-exempt bonds, mortgages, and long-term corporate and government bonds.

At the start of 1962, however, the banks did an abrupt about-face and pushed money heavily into longer-term investments—especially tax-exempt bonds and home mortgages—bringing the yields on these instruments sharply downward and helping to spur construction of homes and new state and municipal capital works projects.

What brought about this change? It was an unexpected result of a rise from 3 to 4 percent in the ceiling on the rate banks could pay for time and savings deposits. When this rate ceiling rose, a great many banks increased the rates they paid savers, to compete against savings banks and savings and loan associations and also to match the rates newly posted by other commercial banks. By themselves the higher rates paid on savings deposits by no means meant that banks could charge more for loans or investments. Lending rates and investment yields are set by the marketplace. No bank, if it expects to keep its customers at times when other lending institutions are not raising their charges, can raise lending charges simply because it wants to offset higher interest costs on savings. Since money was not tight in 1962, there was no economic reason for interest rates on loans and investments to rise, so, as banks started paying more for savings, they had to operate with a smaller margin between rates charged and rates earned.

Faced with this profit squeeze, bank managements looked at their investment officers sitting calmly with the liquid portfolios they had been building since 1960, and felt that here was one area in which new income could be found to boost bank profits. Thus, when the profit squeeze made each additional dollar of income of more significance to the banker (one might even say that the marginal utility of a dollar of income rose), the banks switched from emphasizing liquidity to emphasizing profitability in investment planning.

Ironically, then, while the rates paid to savers rose, the banks became so aggressive in mortgage lending and in buying longer-term municipal bonds that yields on these securities actually fell and, in falling, helped housing and municipal construction, thereby assisting the economy to continue its recovery from the 1960 recession. There is no doubt that the banks' aggressiveness in making longer-term mortgage loans and investments in 1962 and 1963 to fight the profit squeeze contributed considerably to the economy's expansion in the first half of the 1960s, an expansion of record length.

The Federal Reserve itself did a great deal to help this expansion by concentrating its open-market buying in the longer-maturity sector of the government bond market so that yields on long-term securities of all types fell and new borrowing and spending were encouraged. However, the most important factor spurring the economic advance still appears to have been the new aggressiveness of the commercial banks in their lending and investing policies.

Conversely, after the credit crunch of 1973 and 1974, when many younger bankers who had not previously experienced large volumes of loan losses saw many of their credits, especially in the real estate field, go sour, a tone of conservatism descended on the banking industry. The result was a strong emphasis on liquidity and a refusal to push aggressively into long-term investments as loan demands weakened. The banking industry's own conservatism in investment policy thus intensified the economic decline that developed in that period, thereby helping to bring about the worst recession in the United States since the Great Depression of the 1930s.

How can a student of banking come to a conclusion about the function of the investment officer in periods of recession? The officer is torn between liquidity and profitability. There is no sure way of motivating him to move into longer-term investments, and when he stays short, the spillover effect has some impact on the economy. But when he does make longer-term investments, he is of major importance in helping the Federal Reserve achieve the aims of easy money, just as the loan officer helps when he lowers interest rates and becomes more aggressive and imaginative in his lending operations.

6

The Bank's Reaction to Tight Money

The previous chapter looked at the actions of bank lending and investing officers in periods of credit ease. It is now time to look at the banker's reaction in periods of credit restraint, and thus at the role the bank plays in transmitting this restraint to the economy.

As economic activity intensifies and the economy starts to gain strength, the bank feels pressure on its money position in two ways. First, demand for bank loans increases as the economy picks up steam, and second, the Federal Reserve becomes less generous in providing the banking system with new reserves, since the economy no longer needs as much monetary stimulus.

Of course, as a general rule the process is slow in developing, and the bank does not switch overnight from facing easy money to facing credit restraint. Yet slow as this tightening may be, the banks have built in cushioning devices to make the impact of the tightening of credit even more gentle on their borrowing customers than it is on themselves.

The bank's reaction to tightening credit conditions is in many ways the reverse of its reaction to easing of monetary availability. First it becomes somewhat more restrictive in its lending policies and loan terms, turning down new loans it considers marginal in credit-worthiness and beginning to shun loan requests from companies that do not have a solid deposit relationship with the bank. Then it begins to tighten up on its interest rate terms indirectly. This is done by becoming more strict about the percentage of compensating balances the business borrower must keep behind his loans, and by reducing the number of customers entitled to what is called the *prime rate,* the lowest lending rate, which is available only to top-quality borrowers. This step raises the interest rates paid by some borrowers without resorting to a general rise in the bank's overall interest rate structure.

Meanwhile, the banker tries to get more money to lend, so that he can meet the growing demands of his business and individual customers for credit accommodation. In large part, customers maintain their deposit relationships with the bank for the purpose of insuring that the bank will accommodate them when credit becomes scarce. The alternative fund source—the money and capital markets—are impersonal and begin to dry up as soon as investors feel the impact of tight money and reduce their purchases of securities offered there.

To obtain more lendable funds, the banker naturally turns to his investment officer and tells him to start liquidating investments.

If the investment officer has guessed the trend of the business cycle fairly successfully, he will have maintained the liquidity of the investment portfolio and will have a considerable volume of securities maturing in the near future, which he can redeem at their par value.

However, since no bank worth its salt is so conservative in recessions as to keep all its investment funds in liquid securities that mature every few months, to a greater or lesser extent every bank must sell securities before they mature to meet rising loan demands. The investment officer sells securities and takes his capital losses if interest rates have started rising, so that the bank can have more money to lend to its borrowing customers.

Why is a bank willing to take losses on its investments in order to make more loans? On a strict immediate-dollars-and-cents basis, the bank will do this if it feels that over the life of the new loans being placed on its books it will earn more than enough to cover both the future interest forgone by the sale of the bond and also the capital loss accepted in the process of selling the bond in a market of rising interest rates.

The opportunity to earn more on a loan than is sacrificed by the sale of an investment is more frequent than might appear. It must be remembered that if the loan is to an individual, it will probably earn for the bank attractive installment loan rates. If the loan is to a business firm, the bank gets a compensating balance from the borrower, which helps improve the profitability of the loan. Whether the loan is made to a local business or a local individual, or is used to finance a local home, it will help the local economy expand and so also help the bank grow.

Moreover, if the bank does not make the loan requested by a depositor, the customer might well take his deposit to another bank, and the bank would be worse off to that extent.

Thus, the banker expects that immediately, or in the long run, the return from making a loan will be well above the stated interest rate on it. In most instances this will make the return more than adequate to offset the loss of interest on the investment that was sold and the capital loss on the investment's sale.

Another contributing factor is that the Internal Revenue Service makes it more palatable for banks to take the capital losses necessary in the switch from investments to loans during periods of improving business activity. Because, unlike all other businesses and all individuals, in calculating tax liability commercial banks are allowed to deduct all losses on both long-term and short-term securities from normal operating income. This means that if a bank is in the 50-percent federal tax bracket, the Federal Government absorbs one-half the loss the bank takes in the sale of its securities to meet loan demands.

As an offset, however, commercial banks comprise the only industry bound to normal taxation on capital gains, instead of being subject to the lower capital gains taxes that other business firms and individuals are allowed to pay.

But it must be recalled that banks treat investments as a residual use of funds and thus are more likely to take a loss on them than a profit. As a result, the banks are happy to accept this more onerous tax treatment of capital gains to get the more generous handling of their capital losses.

And this mitigation of the after-tax loss in selling bonds as loan demands rise helps banks carry out their function of middlemen in the transmission of credit policy who must move money from investments to local loans and back again, depending upon the need of the economy.

Even if the tax advantage and the corollary income from lending did not offset fully the cost of moving from investments into loans, the bank would still try to shift as much as possible from the investment to the loan portfolio. Lending, after all, is the function of the bank, and the bank that cannot accommodate its borrowing customers in times of credit stringency is going to find that it has far fewer customers left to serve as time passes. The function of the bank is lending, and the banker insulates his borrowers from the impact of tight money as much as he can by reducing his investment portfolio so that he can accommodate his borrowing customers.

The Lock-in Effect

There is a limit to how far a bank can go in increasing loans by reducing holdings of investments. Even though loans provide corollary income over and above the stated interest rate and even though the present tax law allows the bank to deduct a good part of its losses on the sale of investments from normal operating income subject to taxes, as the economy expands a point is reached where the bank no longer converts investments into loans. This limit is reached either when the loss inherent in further reductions in investments is just too great, or when the bank has no investments left in its portfolio other than those comprising part of its secondary reserves of liquidity.

It is easy to see how a bank can reach a point at which the loss from further security sales could well exceed present and future profit obtainable from lending the proceeds. As the economy grows, interest rates will move upward and bond prices downward. Furthermore, the banker is likely to find that losses on his sales of securities steadily increase as time passes, even if interest rate levels in the economy advance awhile and then remain steady at the new higher levels. Unless a banker expects the boom to be exceedingly strong and long lasting, he is likely to reduce his holdings of short-term investments first and only then move into selling longer- and longer-maturity securities if the pressure for funds from the lending officers continues. His reasoning is this: Even though the prices of all bonds decline as interest rates rise, the price of longer-maturity bonds declines far more than the price of short-term ones, to match the same increase in market yields.

The reason for this can be quickly explained by an example. Supposing there are two bonds, both with coupons at 4 percent and both selling at $1000, one of which matures in half a year while the other matures in twenty years. Now let us assume that interest rates rise in the open market so much that both must offer a 6-percent yield to find any buyers. Both, of course, will decline in price, but the bond maturing in six months will not need to decline much in price, because the buyer knows that he will get par value, or $1000, back in six months. Any decline in the bond's price will give the new buyer a capital gain, which he will realize in six months. With a capital gain to be realized in six months, it will not take much of a decline in price to make his 4-percent coupon plus the capital gain give him a total yield equivalent to 2 percent more than the bond offered at par. The twenty-year bond, however, will have to fall much further in price to offer a 6-percent yield. Its new buyer will not realize his capital gain on the difference between the new low price and its par value of $1000 for twenty years. The impact on the bond's annual yield of any capital gain it earns is spread over twenty years, and so even a sharp decline in price will not add much to the bond's effective annual yield through the capital gain. Most of the rise in yield to 6 percent must be generated by lowering the market price, until the $40 annual interest coupon by itself, without the capital gain benefit, reflects almost a 6-percent yield. Specifically, whereas the six-month bond would have to decline from $1000 to $990.30 to bring its yield up to 6 percent, the twenty-year bond would have to decline in price from $1000 to $768.90 to accomplish the same result.

When there is a boom, unless a banker had expected at the beginning that it was going to be of extremely long duration, he would have been tempted to sell short-term securities first as the economy expanded, since the decline in the price of these would have been less than on longer securities for a given rise in interest rates. Then, as he used up his shorter-term investments, even if interest rates did not continue to rise, he would find himself forced to take larger and larger capital losses as he sold longer- and longer-term investments, if the bank's loan demand continued strong. If interest rates continued to rise on top of this, pushing bond prices down further, his losses would be even more serious.

Thus, the point is often reached by commercial banks at which they do not find it possible from the point of overall long-range profitability to sell any more investment securities. The loan income—immediate and long range—that would accrue from converting these funds from investments to loans would not be able to cover the losses involved on the sale. At this point a bank is considered "locked in" with its investments, and it can no longer turn to their sale as a source of funds to meet new loan demand; although some banks feel they can never reach the point at which the loss from a security sale exceeds the long-range loss of income that results from turning down a good borrowing customer or prospect.

Before a bank reaches the point at which it is locked in in its investment portfolio, it does, of course, raise interest rates on loans, which helps compensate for the increased capital losses it must accept in converting investments into lendable funds; but the rise in bank lending rates is restricted by usury laws, by traditional ceilings on what bank customers will pay, and by competition from other banks and from other lending institutions that may not be experiencing such tight credit conditions. Loan rate increases are not a foolproof escape hatch.

Yet the day when the bank is locked in with its investment portfolio is postponed to a considerable degree by the bank's ability to raise lending rates. The rise in bank lending charges as a result of the growing tightness of credit is one way in which the economy is restrained when the Federal Reserve wants economic activity curtailed.

Rate Versus Availability

When the Federal Reserve reduces the availability of bank reserves during a period of improving business conditions, there are several ways in which this reduced availability is reflected in higher interest rates.

First, as business and individual demands for funds pick up, while reserves are made less available, interest rates in the money and capital markets start to advance, simply as a result of the nascent supply-demand pinch. Then, banks start selling securities to meet rising loan demands, and this puts added pressure on investment markets because the increased supply of bonds on the market caused by bank sales to obtain lendable funds pushes bond prices down and interest rates up further.

Finally, and generally after a time lag, banks start raising their lending charges and becoming more strict about compensating balance requirements, as a means of allocating the smaller volume of funds available for lending and as another means of compensating for the capital losses involved in selling securities.

Interest rates rise, both on loans and on investments, which reduces the demand for credit to a degree and helps achieve the Federal Reserve's aim of dampening the rise in economic activity.

However, whereas higher interest rates are to some extent effective in reducing borrowing and spending and thus in avoiding the growth of inflationary pressure at times when the economy's productive facilities are being taxed by the demands being made on them, it must be concluded that high interest rates are almost as ineffective in discouraging some types of borrowing as low interest rates are in encouraging a rise in certain types of borrowing and spending.

To be sure, when interest rates on mortgages rise sharply, people are discouraged from buying houses, and builders of houses become less optimistic over the prospects for sales; and since state and municipal government units must pay for most facilities they construct through collection of tax revenues from an electorate notoriously opposed to higher taxes, they too are sensitive to interest rates, and often postpone borrowing and spending when they feel that interest rate levels are high and will be lower later.

As for individuals who borrow through installment loans, the interest rate level is not much of a deterrent. As we have indicated, individuals are more concerned with how much of each week's income will be absorbed in meeting service charges than in how long the debt will run and consequently in how much effective interest they must pay.

Similarly, since most business capital projects and other activities for which funds are borrowed from banks must be expected to earn at least triple the bank lending charge before they are even considered, any reasonable rise in bank lending charges will not discourage such borrowing. And because of usury laws and traditional interest rate ceilings, it is exceedingly unlikely that bank lending rates will rise so much as to narrow sharply the margin between what business borrowers expect to earn on their investment and what they must pay the bank for the money they need. Moreover, bank borrowing charges are tax deductible, and this further lessens the impact on business of higher bank loan rates.

This should make it clearer why a rise in bank lending charges is likely to discourage only the most marginal of business borrowing requests, those which should undoubtedly be refused anyway because of the dubious chance of successful use of the funds.

But if higher interest rates on money and capital market instruments and on loans do not discourage borrowing by businesses or individuals, how does credit control become effective? The answer is that credit control's main impact on the economy is not primarily through the rise in rates for borrowing from banks and the money and capital markets; it is through the restraints on availability of funds that make it impossible for potential borrowers to have their credit request accommodated.

Even though the commercial banks make it their aim to provide credit accommodation for as many of their customers as possible, they find that they run out of lendable funds in periods when Federal Reserve restraints are making money tight. To be sure, the banks generally are able to hold out for quite a while on lending, because as the function of the bank is to lend it converts as many as possible of its own money- and capital-market investments into cash so that there will be money available to lend. In this regard, the commercial banks serve as a cushion, moderating and delaying the impact of tighter money on their customers.

However, commercial banks find that after a time they can no longer obtain funds to lend. Either they reach the point at which the lock-in effect prevents them from further conversion of investments to loans without unduly sacrificing the earnings potential of the bank, or else they reach the point at which they have converted all the securities in their investment accounts into lendable cash except those which must be maintained as part of their secondary reserves.

This is the main means by which the impact of tight money is passed through the banks and to the economy. It is not done through the bank's saying to its customer, "I have to charge you more for this loan," because the customer frequently is glad to pay for accommodation. It is accomplished by the banker reporting to his potential borrower, "I just do not have the money to lend you at any rate. Therefore I have to turn down your loan request."

Later on we shall examine the concept of *liability management*, a technique utilized by major banks to try to circumvent credit restraint. Through this policy, these aggressive banks have found it possible at times to meet all loan demands by going into the money market and paying whatever interest rate was necessary to attract enough time deposits, Eurodollars, and Federal Funds to obtain all the funds they needed.

But even this procedure, although pushing up interest rates and distorting fund flows among banks, does not weaken the Federal Reserve's power over the economy. All the aggressive liability managers have been able to do is to attract money away from other banks. There is no way that one bank can get more deposits and reserves without having some other bank lose an equivalent amount, if the Federal Reserve is not allowing reserve growth. All deposit money is inside the banking system, and one bank's gain must be another bank's loss, unless the Fed allows creation of more reserves and more deposit money.

Thus one bank may be able to accommodate its customers, at a high price to itself and possibly to them. But the banking system as a whole will still have to turn down just as large a number of requests for loans when the Fed tightens credit whether or not some banks are able to buy their way out of this restraint.

Conclusion

The significance of this allocation process cannot be underestimated. Instead of having the Federal Reserve or the government allocate funds and interfere directly in the operations of financial institutions and the workings of the economy, the Federal Reserve uses the indirect approach of affecting the bank reserve positions. This in turn has an impact on rates and availability of funds in the money and capital markets because the banks sell securities to meet loan demands. Equally important, it slowly but surely limits the banks' ability to lend money to customers, so that the banks have to allocate credit among their potential borrowers, thereby further reducing spending in the economy.

The important aspect of this to a free-enterprise economy is that the banks themselves, rather than a governmental body, determine fund allocation.

Banks try to a considerable degree to allocate their available funds to meet the loan requests that they feel are in the best interest of the economy at the time. In a period of tight money, banks generally will be more receptive to requests for loans for projects that will expand the nation's productive facilities than they will be to loan requests to finance the takeover of a corporation or the speculative purchase of inventory. Bankers also help make the allocation process work by encouraging borrowers to postpone projects until a later date, when the economy will be aided rather than overexpanded by this expenditure, and by inducing potential borrowers to whittle down the size of their borrowing requests. Furthermore, bankers use periods of tight money to upgrade the quality of their loans by refusing borrowing requests that are more marginal than others.

The loan for speculation, the loan for takeover of a company, the project that can be deferred, and the more marginal loan request are, of course, the very areas where it would appear that bank credit should be denied at times when the nation is operating close to capacity and the provision of credit to meet all loan demands would just bring about inflationary expansion of the money supply. Thus, to considerable extent, fund allocation by the banks at times when money is tight accomplishes what the Federal Reserve would do if it were to interfere in the allocation process.

It must also be remembered that banks are business firms, and as such they also must allocate funds in a tight money period along principles that they feel will maximize the long-run profitability of their institutions.

This, of course, leads to a large volume of complaints. Since profit maximization is the basic long-range goal of the commercial bank, it will virtually always find money for installment lending, no matter how tight credit is. Moreover, it will generally find credit for the better customers, whose accounts are more profitable or whose relationship is otherwise considered exceptionally valuable, at the expense of the accommodation of other customers.

Complaints are frequent that this practice favors established companies over new ones, large business over small, and business and installment borrowing over home lending. Although these complaints are certainly true in many instances, the point that must be remembered is that a credit allocation process has to hurt someone, just as a traffic policeman must force some cars and trucks to wait while permiting others to go ahead.

The fact that these classes of potential borrowers are hurt more than others is the price an economy must pay for free-market decision making about how tight money's effects will be felt. Some borrowing must be restrained if the economy is to avoid inflationary pressures, and less economically free systems of allocation hurt some potential borrowers too. Those who advocate easy money at all times so that all borrowers can be accommodated forget that tight money is a necessary evil in fighting inflation. Allowing every request for credit to be accommodated at a time when the economy cannot produce enough goods and services to meet all these desires to spend will merely result in the bidding upward of the prices of the goods and services that are available, rather than in an increase in production and real wealth.

When free-market allocation of funds hurts some borrowers more than others and the government feels that steps should be taken to mitigate this impact on home construction, small-business borrowing, or other sensitive areas, this mitigation can be done in two ways without giving up the basic allocation structure that makes monetary policy's impact consonant with our free economy. First, the government can guarantee loans in these areas; an example is the Federal Housing Administration's guarantee on home loans that meet certain standards. This means that the private borrower is given the backing of a governmental guarantee, which immediately improves the credit quality of his loan request. Such approval, then, places the borrower's request higher on the list of those projects which lenders will consider. Second, the government can lend money to certain sectors either directly or through its financial agencies. This, too, is merely a way of placing these potential borrowers ahead of others in the line waiting for credit, because the government generally must borrow the money it lends to these groups. What happens is that the government steps into the credit markets in place of these borrowers, and because of its higher credit standing it will be accommodated when credit is tight, whereas other borrowers will not.

What must be remembered is that there is no magic way of increasing the availability of funds when the government steps in to help certain areas in the economy. All that really happens is that it is giving a priority place to the aided group. Some other potential borrower further down the line will now have to be denied credit accommodation because the aided sector of the economy was placed ahead of him in line for the limited supplies of credit that are available.

Be this as it may, the significant conclusion must be this: Whether or not the government offers its credit standing to aid weaker borrowers, the money and capital markets and the banks are engaged in allocating what money is available to those borrowers who they feel offer the lender the best return available relative to the risk that must be taken.

This is how a free-market economy should allocate funds in periods of tight money, when not all potential borrowers can be satisfied. It should be clear by now that the banks, while trying to cushion the impact of tight money on their customers, serve as the necessary middlemen between the Federal Reserve System and the economy, making the process of credit restraint as consonant as possible with the principles of a free economy. The alternative is governmental determination of how credit should be allocated, and one can only wonder what principles, priorities, and precedents would be established if political forces were to replace marketplace decision making in determining who will bear what share of the burden that the fight against inflation imposes on an economy.

7

Barriers to Effective Monetary Policy

While the process of transmitting the impact of monetary policy from the Federal Reserve through the commercial banks to the economy looks rather uneven and inexact as presented above, actually the process is even rougher than that. Institutional barriers inhibit and delay the effective transmission of monetary policy through the banking system to the desired goal of encouraging or discouraging borrowing and spending. Prime among these are the offsetting influence often exerted by fiscal policy and debt management, and the ability of holders of funds to speed up the turnover, or velocity, of money, and thus negate much of the impact of tighter money.

Fiscal Policy and Debt Management

As has been indicated above, fiscal policy and debt management work hand-in-glove. When there is a fiscal deficit, it is up to the Treasury, as the manager of the public debt, to borrow enough to fill the gap between what the Congress has spent and what it has collected in taxes. When there is a surplus, the Treasury has the principal say in how that surplus will be utilized to retire debt outstanding.

If fiscal policy were so exercised that it always served as a contracyclical force—helping the economy recover from recessions and curbing spending in booms—there would be fiscal deficits in recessions and fiscal surpluses in booms. In debt management, in recessions the Treasury would finance the debt by selling securities to commercial banks—so that they would be paid for through the creation of new deposit money; in booms it would retire debt held by banks—so that the money supply would contract, or at least rise much more slowly, to help dampen spending activity.

Fiscal policy is seldom that well attuned to the needs of the economy. Whereas it is usual to find deficits in recessions, deficit financing is fairly typical in booms as well. The reason is that congressmen, being political beings, are always more prone to favor low taxes and increased government spending than vice versa. Fiscal policy is usually an expansionary force in both booms and recessions, with the result that monetary policy must bear the brunt of restraining the economy in boom periods.

Debt management without appropriate fiscal policy cannot be a major contracyclical force. Yet it does play a major role in determining whether a fiscal deficit will have an expansionary impact on the economy or whether it will be neutral, and whether a fiscal surplus will be contracting or neutral. The Treasury can determine whether the securities issued will be of the type banks buy, with payment made by creating new deposit money, or of the kind individuals and financial intermediaries buy, with payment made by utilizing funds that otherwise would be spent elsewhere.

Similarly, although the Treasury cannot retire debt or force lenders to take their money back, it can have a role in determining whose securities will be retired by its choice of what types of securities to issue as replacement when outstanding securities mature. For example, if it desires bank-held debt to decline, as debt matures the Treasury will concentrate its refunding on the types of securities that are bought by individuals and not by banks.

The Treasury has methods of inducing banks to buy securities at certain times and of interesting nonbank institutions and individuals in buying them at other times. The Treasury can make certain issues ineligible for banks, as it does with savings bonds, or it can limit to a relatively small amount the share of an issue that a bank may hold. It can also try to induce financial intermediaries to buy certain issues by letting them pay for them on an installment basis as new savings money comes into them over a period. However, the Treasury's main method of selecting buyers for the securities it offers is through its maturity scheduling on its debt.

The Treasury knows that for commercial banks investments have two purposes, secondary reserves for liquidity and investments for income when loan demands are weak. It knows that if it wants to get banks to buy its securities for their secondary reserves, it must offer short-term obligations, because no bank will hold long-maturity issues as part of its liquidity position, since in times of high interest rates they cannot be converted into cash quickly without loss. The Treasury also knows that most aggressive banks avoid including long-term government issues in their investment accounts as well, because, although the investment account does not need to offer liquidity, it must provide the bank with the highest return possible. When banks are willing to sacrifice liquidity and they seek high yield in investment purchases, they find that much higher after-tax return can be obtained in state and municipal bonds, which are exempt from federal income taxes, than in U.S. government obligations of similar maturity, with only a modest increase in risk of default. Banks find that some corporate bonds, private bonds insured by the U.S. government, and bonds sold by agencies of the government to obtain money for lending as special credit accommodation to certain areas of the economy (such as housing, farming, and savings and loan associations) also offer considerably higher returns than U.S. government obligations with minimal sacrifice of quality.[1]

Just as a *yield curve* shows the available choices among various combinations of yield and maturity in securities of the same quality, a *yield spread* shows the available choices among securities of differing quality. By placing on the same chart the yield curves for various securities, the investor can see the differences in yield

---

[1] Commercial banks keep some U.S. government obligations as "pledged securities" which back the deposits of various state and local governments and some other governmental units. These government bodies require the pledging of securities so that the full proceeds from the sale of these securities will be available to cover their deposits in case the bank fails. This in effect gives these public depositors a priority position over that of other depositors in claiming bank assets in periods of trouble.

Since the deposits these pledged securities back usually are maintained for long time periods, the banks do not look for liquidity in the securities they hold as pledges, and they will often hold long-term U.S. government obligations as pledged assets to gain yields higher than short-term government securities usually offer. But aggressive banks hold few or no long-term U.S. government securities other than as pledged assets.

between different types of securities at all maturity ranges. The added yield made available by switching from one security to a lower-quality one of the same maturity might more than compensate for the lower quality and justify sacrificing quality for yield; conversely, at any specific maturity position the yield spread might be so narrow between two types of securities that a small sacrifice in yield might result in a considerable improvement in quality and justify sacrificing yield for quality.

A typical yield spread is shown in Figure 6. This yield spread shows that the bank investment officer can obtain a higher yield on corporate securities and on U.S. government agency securities than on direct obligations of the U.S. government. Although the yields on tax-exempt state and municipal securities are below those of all other issues, it must be remembered that on an after-tax equivalent basis, these, too, offer higher yields than U.S. government securities to an institution or individual in the tax bracket of the typical commercial bank.

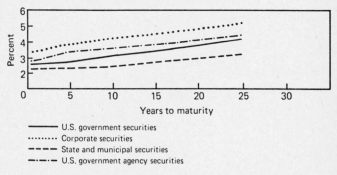

Figure 6   A Typical Yield Spread

Whether the yield spread shows the investor opportunities to switch from one type of security to another cannot, of course, be determined by the chart itself. This depends solely on the investor's present evaluation of just how much additional risk, if any, he is willing to take for an additional increment of yield.

Going back to debt management, on the basis of usual yield spreads, many aggressive banks shun longer-term governments for their investment accounts, and all banks refuse to hold long governments in their secondary reserves. The Treasury knows, then, that when it wants to sell securities to commercial banks, it must concentrate on short-term and at most intermediate-term maturity obligations.

Nonbank financial institutions, on the other hand, are more aggressive in their government security purchases. Even though there is a growing hesitancy among all financial institutions in buying long-term U.S. government obligations, because of the higher yields available on other long-term securities, they are still somewhat attractive to financial intermediaries. These institutions need to hold some of their assets as riskless investments, and so they buy some U.S. government obligations. To many intermediaries, long governments are preferable to short-term governments, because long-term governments generally offer higher yields than short-terms do, and liquidity is not very important to these buyers. Insurance companies and pension funds know much better than banks how long their money will stay with them. They do not know which of their policyholders and pensioners will die each year, but they do have an adequate actuarial indication of how many will die and therefore of what their fund outflow status will be. Thus they buy longer-term governments, as do some savings banks and other financial intermediaries that also have considerably greater stability in the rate of their money input and outflow than commercial banks.

If the Treasury planned its debt management policy to be completely consonant with contracyclical monetary policy, it would rely on short-term securities in recessions, since banks buy them and pay for them mainly by creating new money, whereas it would rely on long-term securities in booms, since these would be paid for by the sopping up of some of the lendable funds held by financial intermediaries and those individuals who also are attracted to long-term government securities.

It can be quickly shown, however, that this, although in the best interest of a sound contracyclical policy, would be in direct conflict with the other aim of the Treasury, that of financing the national debt at the lowest possible interest cost.

In a recession, when interest rates are low, if the Treasury wants low-cost financing, it is well advised to finance its debt with long-term securities. By doing so it locks itself in with the low borrowing rates for a long period in the same way as a buyer of beer would want to buy several cases and store them away at a time when beer prices are exceptionally low.

Contrarily, in a boom, when interest rates are high the Treasury's aim of financing the national debt at the lowest cost is best served by selling short-term securities. In this way the Treasury will be paying today's high interest rates only for a short period, and it will be able to refund its debt at lower borrowing cost later. In this regard, the Treasury is like a beer consumer who buys only enough to quench one small thirst at a time when beer prices are unusually high.

The dilemma the Treasury faces between choosing a debt management policy that is cheapest for the taxpayers and one that is in the best interest of a stable economy is summarized in Figure 7.

In principle, cheap debt management works in direct opposition to the aims of monetary policy instead of in consort with it.

Although there have been long periods in which the Treasury's debt management policy has been a hindrance to effective monetary policy—involving selling short-term securities in booms and long-term obligations in recessions—since the sharp 1958 bond market decline, the Treasury has been more of an ally of the Federal Reserve. The paucity of buyers for treasury obligations in mid-1958 showed the Treasury that it was in the best interest of effective debt management to have a dollar of stable value rather than to have lower-cost borrowing. When the value of the dollar declines, so does the attractiveness of fixed-income securities, whose interest and principal value are fixed in dollar terms and do not increase to match the rising cost of living and the erosion of the dollar's value.

	In recessions	In booms
For lowest cost debt management, Treasury would like to sell:	Long securities	Short securities
For debt management consonant with the aims of monetary policy, Federal Reserve would like Treasury to sell:	Short securities	Long securities

Figure 7   Aims of Debt Management Versus Monetary Policy over the Business Cycle

Debt management policy in recent years consequently has been more of a friend of Federal Reserve policy than an opponent of it, because the Treasury has considered the fight for economic stability as an integral part of debt management.

Liquidity

As an ally of the Federal Reserve in furthering sustainable noninflationary economic growth, the Treasury has had to face another problem as important as who buys government bonds. This is the avoidance of having too many short-term liquid securities available on the market.

For the Treasury to have much of its financing consist of short-term, liquid securities would be the path of least resistance in debt management. As shown above, there is much more of a market for short-term treasury obligations than for longer ones. Short-term treasury securities are held by banks as the basis of their secondary reserves. They are purchased by nonfinancial corporations that are looking to invest money being held for tax payments or for dividend distribution on certain dates in the near future in money market investments of maximum safety. Also, financial intermediaries, and especially savings banks and savings and loan associations, need some short-term government securities as a secondary reserve. Even though these intermediaries have greater deposit stability than banks, they need some liquidity so that they can meet requests for withdrawal of savings above their expected average without having to sell mortgages and other long-term investments in a hurry.

On the other hand, the market for longer-term government obligations is fairly thin. Banks do not purchase them in any quantity, and the institutions and individuals that do buy long-term securities, although they hold some long governments, frequently prefer to buy other investments that are of lower quality than U.S. government obligations but more than compensate for this through higher yields. Thus, it is far easier for the Treasury to rely on short-term securities than on longer ones.

Moreover, each day every outstanding Treasury security moves one day closer to maturity, so the Treasury faces a terrific house-keeping problem of continually refinancing securities out into longer-term maturities to prevent its average debt maturity from becoming shorter day by day.

Yet the Treasury and the Federal Reserve dislike seeing the national debt become ever shorter in maturity, because that increases the liquidity of the economy, which in turn offsets the effectiveness of Federal Reserve credit-restraining actions.

Excess liquidity in the economy presents a challenge to the effectiveness of monetary policy in this manner. When the public has large holdings of long-term government securities, and interest rates start to rise, most of the holders are forced to maintain their positions, since nonbanks as well as banks can get locked in with securities on which a serious capital loss has to be realized if they are sold.

When a great volume of short-term securities is held in portfolios—as is the case when the Treasury relies on the easy path in debt management—these investors are not locked in. Rather, they know that either they can take their modest losses and sell out (short-term securities decline much less in price than long-term issues, given an identical rise in interest rate levels), or they can wait to maturity to get par value for their investments, because they do not have to wait long. Holders of short-term securities can get their money back quickly in a period of credit restraint, and they can put it into other investments or spend it. Holders of short-term liquid instruments thus find that their spending activity is just as immune to the impact of credit control as are the drinking activities of a man who starts out a temporary period of national prohibition with several hundred kegs of his favorite spirits in his cellar. This is one way in which the availability of a large volume of short-term securities can frustrate the Federal Reserve's efforts to restrain spending in the economy.

When the holders of maturing short-term securities get their money back, the government, as the original borrower of this money, must find new fund sources, and as it seeks new funds, it causes a second moderation of the effectiveness of monetary policy. To understand how this occurs, it is necessary to understand the role of monetary velocity.

Monetary Velocity

It may be recalled that earlier in the book we stated that a rise in the velocity of turnover of money has just as much of an impact on spending in the economy as would a proportional rise in the quantity of money available. This can be symbolized by the Equation of Exchange, $MV = PT$: *M*oney supply times the *V*elocity of turnover of money equals the *P*rices of all goods and services sold times the physical volume of *T*ransactions of goods and services sold.

That speeded velocity of money is a direct substitute for a rising quantity of money can be quickly demonstrated. If fifty men are seated in a circle, and each is told he is going to sell his tie to the man on his left for $1, this transaction can be accomplished in one of two ways. First, one man can take a dollar from his pocket and pass it to the next in payment for the second man's tie. The second man then can pass that dollar to the third, and so on, until the one dollar has turned over fifty times and financed the sale of fifty ties. Second, each man can stand up, take a dollar from his pocket, and pass it to the left at the same time as he passes his tie to the right, in which case $50 will have turned over to finance the sale of fifty ties, each dollar turning over only once. Thus the Equation of Exchange is $50 \times 1 V = \$1 \times 50$ *ties* (when turnover is once), or $1 \times 50 V = \$1 \times 50$ *ties* (when the same dollar moves through the entire room).

The impact of $MV = PT$ on monetary policy comes from the fact that the Federal Reserve can influence only *M*, the money supply. It has no direct control over *V*, or velocity of money in the public's hands. There is nothing the Federal Reserve can do directly to influence hoarding of money or to change the rate at which people utilize their demand deposits in commercial banks.

On the other hand, velocity of money can be and is influenced by the rate of interest in the economy, because as interest rates rise people value money more and use it more rapidly and effectively than when the income sacrificed by leaving it idle in hoards or in bank accounts is much less.

One might conclude that the Federal Reserve could influence velocity of money by changing the availability of money and thus influencing the interest rate level; but a closer examination will show that there is no way in which the Federal Reserve can influence monetary velocity without allowing the quantity of money to move in the opposite direction from that desired.

To illustrate. If the Federal Reserve worried about the rise in velocity of money and the inflationary implications thereof, it could slow the turnover by only one means: giving the banks more reserves, so that supply of money would rise, interest rates would fall, and holders of money would be less anxious to spend their cash and deposits. This, obviously, would hurt rather than help. The rise in the money supply necessary to slow monetary velocity would cause at least as much inflationary pressure as, and probably far more of it than, the slowed deposit velocity would prevent. If the Federal Reserve were eager to spur turnover of money, its only way of achieving this would be to tighten credit, so that the liquidity preference, or preference of the individual to hold cash, would be reduced and he would spend his money faster. But again, the tightening of credit would undoubtedly restrain the economy far more than the increased velocity would expand it.

Thus, a rise in monetary velocity partly offsets and partly cushions the impact of tight money; conversely, the reduction in turnover of deposits lessens the stimulating influence of an increase in the money supply.

Returning to debt management, then, it can now be made clear why a large supply of liquidity instruments has a dual impact on spending. First, it gives the holders of these liquid instruments a chance to turn them in for cash at maturity with no loss in asset value, so that they can continue with their spending plans in the face of monetary restraint; moreover, as liquid government securities are redeemed on maturity, the government must refund its debt by borrowing more from someone else, except in the improbable circumstance of a fiscal surplus. And with the holders of short-term government securities turning them in for cash, the Treasury must raise the rate of interest it offers on new securities, because only in this way can it encourage holders of idle cash and idle bank deposits to place their money into the new securities it must sell to replace the maturing issues. This process, of course, brings heightened velocity of money, which is the second offset to the effectiveness of Federal Reserve policy resulting from availability of large amounts of liquid instruments.

In recent years the Treasury has done all it can to keep stretching the average maturity of outstanding issues, despite the 4¼-percent ceiling on long Treasury securities mentioned above, so that the liquidity of the economy would not frustrate the aims of monetary policy. It has done this by selling long bonds when it can and by frequently using the technique of *advance refunding.* The aim of this technique is to entice holders of securities that are nearing maturity and thus that offer the holder a great deal of liquidity an attractive premium above the going market price for these securities if they will "trade them in" for new, longer-term securities that the Treasury is issuing.

Institutional Forces in Velocity

The Federal Reserve is not completely helpless with regard to increased velocity of money. Although it can do nothing to slow the velocity of money, it can offset the impact of this speeded turnover of bank deposits and cash. The method available is rather simple. If increased velocity of money reduces the impact of a certain amount of credit tightening, all the Federal Reserve does is tighten credit further, to offset the increased velocity.

This is as it should be; the Federal Reserve's aim is not a specific level of money supply, but rather to control the amount of spending in the economy. It is concerned with the $M \times V$ force in the Equation of Exchange, not just the money supply (M) factor, and if it seems that, owing to increased monetary velocity, $M \times V$ is getting too large for the available goods and services (T) and that this can only lead to a rise in prices (P), it merely pulls back on the one factor it can influence, the money supply (M), until $M \times V$ is again consonant with the capacity of the nation.

To the commercial banks, however, this has quite a serious impact. Whereas the economy at large looks on M and V as interchangeable and concerns itself mainly with the total level of spending, the level of unemployment of manpower and materials, and the price level, to the commercial banks the Federal Reserve's restraint on M to offset a rise in V has serious consequences on profits.

To the bank M and V are by no means interchangeable. M is money supply, basically, demand deposits—and demand deposits are the most profitable source of bank funds, since no interest is paid on them. V, or velocity, to a bank means work; the speeded turnover of deposits means more checks to clear, more items to post to bank statements, and more details of all kinds to handle. When velocity of money rises and the Federal Reserve reacts by restricting the growth of the money supply, the banks are doubly hurt: they are doing more work in handling the more rapid turnover of deposits, and yet instead of their being compensated for the higher costs involved, the Federal Reserve reacts by letting their most profitable lifeblood, demand deposits, grow more slowly. To the Federal Reserve this is the logical approach that must be taken to keep rising velocity from frustrating monetary policy; to the bank it is a case of turning the other cheek after one has been hit and then being hit on the second also. (The cost is offset to some degree by higher bank fees to compensate for the higher volume of activity, but not fully.)

Because of the double impact on bank profitability that results from speeded velocity of money, one would think that commercial banks would do all they could to reduce and discourage the turnover of deposits. Yet in actuality commercial banks themselves have been a major force in speeding up the turnover of funds left on deposit, as part of the service offered to business firms in the fight to win their accounts away from other banks.

In order to understand how this speed-up in velocity can be induced by the banks themselves, it must first be remembered that when we examined the balance sheet of the Schmidlap National Bank and Trust Company (Chapter Four) there was a portion of the cash and due-from-banks item that reflected cash items in the process of collection. To review, when a bank customer writes a check on his account and sends it out to pay a bill, the check is deposited in the bank of the check's recipient. The receiving bank does not yet have the use of this money; it must clear the check back to the bank of issue before it gets paid. Even if it turns the check over to its local Federal Reserve bank for clearance, the Federal Reserve will not give the bank "good funds," or an increase in its Federal Reserve deposit that it may use, until one or two days later. The Federal Reserve must have time to clear the check to the bank on which it was written and get its money back from this institution. The receiving bank, in turn, does not give the depositor of the check good funds, or a collected balance, until enough days have passed at least for clearance of the check.

The process of writing checks, then, always leads to double balances on the books of the banks, even though they are netted out in calculating the money supply. If on Monday a man writes a check in New York and mails it to a San Francisco, California company, the recipient in California is not likely to get the check until Friday (unless the payer is the type of eager beaver who pays bills by special delivery mail). The recipient deposits the check on Friday, and since the bank makes him wait for it to clear before letting him write checks on this new increase in his balance, very likely he will not have good funds until Wednesday of the next week at the earliest. Thus, in a nine-day period, both the sender of the funds and the receiver maintain deposits in their banks for the amount of this check. The sender has sent his check to California, and feels that he does not have use of the money any more, even though it is still in his account until the check clears. Neither does the receiver have the use of the money until the nine days pass, and he must keep other money on deposit to meet his financial needs in the meantime.

With new techniques that banks now make available to their customers, however, this double maintenance of the deposit is no longer necessary. Now, the man in New York writes his check and mails it not to San Francisco but to a post office lockbox in New York City. There it is handled by a New York City bank, which wires the funds directly to the California recipient of the money. Instead of receiving the money a week from Wednesday, the California company will have its money on Tuesday—eight days earlier—and need tie up that much less of its other funds in its bank balance. To recapitulate the transaction: The payer of the check gains nothing; he wrote the check Monday and had no further use of the funds. The fact that they are now taken out of his account on Tuesday instead of on the Wednesday of the following week means little to him (unless he is so low in money that he is writing checks without covering funds and hoping that by the time the checks reach the receivers and are cleared through back to his bank he will be able to place enough in the bank to cover them).[2] To his bank, however, it means the loss of this deposit money eight days sooner.

Where has this money gone? It has not gone to the California bank, which now has only as much of a balance of good funds from the California company as it had before. What has happened is that the company using a lockbox and wire transfer of funds now needs to keep that much less money tied up in its checking account and has thus speeded the turnover, or velocity, of its deposit. The freed funds can be used in the company's business or invested in the money market.

Similarly banks now allow some customers to pay bills by drafts rather than checks. It is not necessary to keep any money in the bank to back a draft. Only when the draft comes back to the bank for payment, through the normal check collection process, must the customer immediately sell enough short-term securities or otherwise find enough cash to provide the bank with the funds needed to cover its draft. A draft looks just like a check, except that generally it states "pay through" and the name of the bank, instead of just showing the bank's name in the way a check does. Again, the use of the draft allows a bank's customer to operate with less on deposit and speeds the turnover of money.

Why do banks not only allow such techniques, but also encourage them? The answer is that competition forces them to do it, just as competition is responsible for gasoline price wars, in which gas prices fall but none of the stations involved ends up pumping more gas once all the community's dealers join in the war.[3]

The bank offering the lockbox from New York City says to the California company, "If you give us a small deposit, we will clear your checks faster and help you reduce the amount that you keep in your California bank by a much larger amount than the deposit we demand of you." In effect, though, it is saying, "If you give us a small deposit, we will help you reduce by far more the deposits of a lot of other banks on which checks are written and sent to you."

[2]This is called "playing the float." And because many people operate this way it is making it harder for banks to institute electronic techniques that move money faster than checks do.
[3]This practice was far more common before the oil embargo of 1973–4 than it is today, but the analogy still holds true.

For the one bank offering the lockbox, this is certainly benefi-
cial, but it reduces total deposits in the banking system as a whole.
Once many banks offer lockbox services, then all of them lose
deposits on balance, but they are as helpless in this situation as the
individual dealer is in a gas war; once the war has started he must
either match the low price simply to maintain his own volume or
face a serious decline in business.

Not only are drafts, lockboxes, and wire transfers of funds being
utilized to speed the turnover of deposits and to increase monetary
velocity, but also new electronic techniques are being developed
that are speeding this turnover even more.

Individuals, as indicated above, can now pay bills by telephone
at many banks and thrift institutions. They can more conveniently move demand deposit money into and out of near-money
accounts, such as savings deposits and money-market funds, by a
phone call or by the push of a button on a remote automatic-teller
device or a point-of-sale terminal. Financial institutions are developing methods for automatic deposit of payrolls, dividend checks,
and other routine deposits, and they are offering programs for
automatic payment of routine bills, such as those owed utilities.
In addition the debit card, a magnetically encoded plastic, is being
introduced as a device to be used at convenient locations, such as
grocery stores, to instruct bank computer terminals how to move
the depositor's funds.

Automated clearing houses are also being established, so that
bank computer terminals anywhere in the nation can send electronic instructions to other banks' terminals located anywhere in
the nation. And when this network is fully functioning, it will
markedly reduce the need for the use of paper checks because it
will allow instructions for payment to move electronically from
the initiating depositor to the receiving one, no matter where
either may be.

The check will still be with us. Not all transfers will become
electronic by any means. And many people still will prefer the
check, since it serves as a receipt for payment made and it gives
the user a float time before the money must be in the bank—
something electronic bill-paying eliminates. And those who formerly used the futuristic term "checkless society" have backed
down to accepting the concept of the "less check society."

All these new trends, summarized under the concept of EFTS —Electronic Funds Transfer Services—are having an even greater impact on velocity, or turnover, of money than earlier innovations such as the lockbox caused. And today velocity of money plays a much greater role in determining Federal Reserve credit policy and the amount of money the banks are allowed to create than ever before.

Yet despite these new institutional techniques to speed turnover of money that are making the V in the Equation of Exchange more important at the expense of the M, one major force that has speeded money turnover and reduced the effectiveness of the Federal Reserve has been brought under much better control in recent years. This was the rapid growth of the role of financial intermediaries at the expense of the growth of commercial banks. However, it appears that this trend has now been slowed markedly by the drastic change that has taken place in banking, a turning away from reliance on demand deposits and toward dependence on time and savings deposits as the basic source of bank growth.

As the next chapter will show, although this trend has not slowed the rate of growth of money turnover because of the new techniques summarized under the term EFTS, it has kept the commercial banks from playing a steadily decreasing role on the financial scene and in the American economy.

8

The
Changing
Sources
of Bank
Deposits

$\mathbb{I}$n the two decades following the prohibition in 1933 of payment of interest on demand deposits, most commercial banks were not greatly interested in time and savings deposits.

There were several reasons for this. First, until recent years most commercial banks have been more interested in serving business firms than in serving individuals; it was business that first needed banks and made possible the establishment of profitable banks. This explains why savings banks were established to provide the smaller saver with a repository for his funds and why savings and loan associations were established to provide mortgage money for the home buyer. Banks then preferred to concentrate on providing demand deposit services for businesses instead of trying to develop the savings accounts of individuals.

Second, in historical perspective, the period from 1933 to 1951 was one of extremely low interest rates. From 1933 to 1940 the nation was in the Great Depression, and naturally monetary policy was kept extremely easy to help encourage any borrowing and spending that could be generated. From 1940 to 1945, during World War II, interest rates were kept low to make it less expensive for the Treasury to borrow the money needed to finance the war. This could be done without serious inflationary consequences because powerful direct controls, such as rationing and price controls, were being used to protect the dollar's value from erosion. From 1945 to 1951, interest rates were kept low by deliberate monetary policy for several reasons. First, there was a fear that a new depression would develop, as had occurred after every other major war, and the money managers wanted credit policy as liberal as possible to help avoid this possibility. Second, a great many government securities had been sold to the public during the war.

The Treasury felt that if it allowed interest rates to rise and bond prices consequently to fall, those who had bought government bonds for patriotic reasons would be left with a capital loss for their trouble, new lenders would be discouraged by the falling bond prices, and, of at least equal significance, the government's cost of new borrowing would also soar.

Hence, the United States had over twenty years of credit ease, from the early 1930s to 1951, when the Korean War brought about serious inflationary pressures and necessitated tightening of monetary policy. (The actual tightening came about only after an agreement between the Treasury and the Federal Reserve System, called the Accord of March 4, 1951. By this agreement the Federal Reserve was given full freedom in its open-market operations, and it no longer had to stand ready, as it had in the previous decade, to buy all government securities offered to it at certain minimum prices, which had kept these securities from falling in price and thereby rising in yield.)

As far as the banks were concerned, during the easy money period from the early 1930s until 1946 there was no need to buy time and savings deposits in any quantity, since free excess reserves were plentiful and loan demands were weak. From 1946 to 1951, moreover, there was no real need to buy time and savings deposits because banks could get all the money they wanted by redeeming government securities at supported prices. Most banks hesitated to start buying money in large quantities and preferred to rely on demand deposits, on which no interest is paid. Banks also feared that if they started soliciting time and savings deposits, they would simply be buying back their own demand deposits, thus paying interest on money formerly held free.

This policy of not soliciting time and savings deposits was successful for most banks until the mid-1950s; but following the Treasury-Federal Reserve Accord, and especially following the restoration of convertibility to Western European currencies, interest rates rose and both individual and corporate holders of demand deposits found it worthwhile to look elsewhere for a repository for surplus funds. When interest rates were below 1 percent in the money market, a corporation did not think it worthwhile to invest its excess demand deposit funds in short-term securities, because the bother of investing was much too great for the ½-percent-or-so after-tax return available. Similarly, when savings banks and savings and loan associations offered relatively low rates on savings, many individuals felt it was not worth the effort to take money out of their commercial bank checking accounts and place it into savings deposits in another institution.

The rise in interest rates during the 1950s changed all this. Corporations began to place excess funds into treasury bills and other short-term securities. Individuals became more and more interested in opening accounts in savings banks and savings and loan associations. The commercial banks were faced with a competitive situation different from anything they had experienced in twenty to twenty-five years.

Why Compete?

The first question the commercial bankers had to face was, Why bother to compete for time and savings deposits? Even if the public removes its excess funds from banks and places them into commercial paper sold by corporate borrowers, treasury bills, savings banks, savings and loan associations, or any other form of financial instrument or financial intermediary, the money reverts to a bank demand deposit.

If, for example, an individual feels he has too much in his checking account and decides to place $100 in a savings bank, the transaction is accomplished by his drawing a check on his own commercial bank and depositing it with the savings bank, which in turn places this check in its account at either the same or some other commercial bank. Then, when the savings bank makes a loan to a potential home buyer, it gives him a check on its commercial bank demand deposit, which the home buyer turns over to the seller of the house. This check in turn is likely to be deposited in the house seller's demand deposit in his commercial bank. (If the seller happens to place the check in a savings bank or savings and loan association himself, then one savings-bank- or savings-and-loan-held demand deposit is just replaced by another, and the savings institution receiving the check simply makes a new mortgage loan, which the second home seller is likely to place in his demand deposit account at a commercial bank.)

Thus, when the commercial banks do not compete for time and savings deposits, instead of their losing deposits, the level of demand deposits remains static, because deposits move from one holder to another.

The result is similar when commercial banks do not compete for the money that business firms want to place into interest-bearing securities or time deposits. If a check is written on a bank demand deposit to buy Treasury bills, commercial paper, or some other money market instrument, the seller of these securities places his receipts into a bank demand deposit, and as the receipts are spent, the money moves to someone else's demand deposit.

If the seller of the securities happens to be a commercial bank, demand deposits are destroyed, just as they are created when a bank buys a security. The purchaser of the securities brings down his bank account, while the bank selling the securities gets cash or reserves at Federal Reserve for the securities it sells but no increase in deposits. However, if there is any demand for loan or investment funds, this decline in deposits is only temporary. The new cash and reserves that the selling bank obtains can serve as required reserves to back new deposits, replacing those which were destroyed. Even in this case, the movement of money from bank demand deposits into money market instruments is likely to leave bank demand deposit levels just where they were.

This is why some have argued that the banks should not compete for time and savings deposits, since the money they lose by not competing stays right in the banking system anyway.

A more careful analysis reveals, however, that the banks do have a lot to lose by not competing for time and savings deposits, even though demand deposit levels would stay the same if they did not compete.

One Bank Versus the System

The first problem that banks face when they do not compete for time and savings deposits is the one that faces them when they have the chance to increase their own deposits by speeding the turnover of their customers' deposits in other banks through new techniques such as the lockbox and wire transfer of funds. What is good for one bank may not be good for the banking system.

Although it is true that the banking system as a whole does not lose demand deposits by not competing for time and savings deposit funds, for the individual bank there can be a considerable loss of deposits. If, for example, a man draws on his deposit account with a commercial bank to open a savings account at a savings bank, and if the savings bank uses a different commercial bank as its repository from the one on which the saver drew his check, then the bank on which the check was drawn definitely loses a deposit, even if the banking system does not. Similarly, a bank on which a check is drawn for Treasury bill purchases loses deposits and reserves by not competing to keep the excess funds of its corporate depositors.

To the bank that has lost the money, the loss is not ameliorated by the knowledge that another bank has gained new reserves to use in new lending and investing. Even though the banking system may lose no deposits by not competing for time and savings money, individual banks find they must compete for them at times to avoid loss of deposits to other banking institutions, even when no individual commercial bank is competing for savings.

Far more significant to the whole banking system is the fact that when commercial banks do not compete for time and savings deposits, though the banking system's demand deposit totals do not fall, neither do they rise.

In the examples given earlier in this connection, loans were made and homes were financed, yet the deposits and loan totals of commercial banks remained unchanged. The growth of the economy was financed not by the creation of new bank loans and demand deposits but by the creation of new credit instruments in the form of savings bank deposits and savings and loan shares, which in effect required the ever more rapid turnover of the same amount of commercial bank demand deposits. In other words, the economy was financed by rising velocity of money, or V from the Equation of Exchange, rather than by expansion of M, or the demand deposit component of the active money supply.

The economy grew, but the banks did not. They found themselves staying the same size and doing more and more bookkeeping work, recording and keeping track of this financing of the economy that was accomplished through heightened velocity of money.

This readily explains why even though the money supply—and bank demand deposits, which are the major component of the money supply—should grow about as rapidly as the economy grows, in the 1950s this was not the case. While the economy, as measured by the gross national product (GNP), rose 80 percent, bank demand deposits grew only 21 percent.

The velocity of money speeded up, owing to the banks' unwillingness to compete for time and savings deposits, and as this happened the Federal Reserve had no choice but to restrict the rise in the money supply by tightening the rate of growth of bank reserves and bank demand deposits; it was the rising supply of nonbank credit instruments and the rising velocity of money that played a major role in financing the economic growth of the 1950s, and the Federal Reserve's money managers had to limit the growth of the money supply to keep total money supply times its turnover within the limits of the nation's ability to turn out goods and services.

The Change in Attitude

It would be incorrect to state that the commercial banks changed their minds with regard to solicitation of time and savings deposits because they recognized the impact their unwillingness to compete had on the velocity of money and therefore on demand deposit growth.

The change came about because individual institutions saw their own growth coming at a slower rate than that of their competitors in the savings bank and savings and loan industries. Then, as a few commercial banks started competing for time and savings deposits, they found themselves able not only to prevent or reduce losses of funds to the specialized thrift institutions but also to bring in as savings and time deposits money that formerly resided in demand deposits in other banks. It was not long before a great many other commercial banks were forced into soliciting time and savings deposits, as a weapon against deposit erosion by financial intermediaries and other commercial banks as well.

Yet although this defensive purpose undoubtedly was the original motivation for most banks that started competing for time and savings deposit money, banks in general began to see that they could no longer count on demand deposit growth to provide enough money to meet their loan demands, as was the case in the past.

The fact that the GNP was able to grow four times more rapidly than bank demand deposits certainly worried the individual bank. But the bank could not see by examination of its own operations the whole picture of how the rising velocity of money was forcing the Federal Reserve to slow the rate of monetary growth, since the individual bank only receives deposit funds and lends them out. However, the banks could see certain serious trends, once interest rates started to rise in the 1950s:

1. Individuals were beginning to keep demand deposits to a minimum, placing their extra funds in savings banks and savings and loan associations.

2. Corporate treasurers were doing the same thing—reducing their demand deposits to a minimum and utilizing the rest of their balances to buy money market securities.

3. The newer techniques, such as the draft and the lockbox, were reducing the amount of deposits that the banks held as part of *float* time (the time between the writing of a check and its clearance, during which the writer feels he has spent his deposit but the bank still has the use of the funds because the writer's check has not yet cleared). As checks were cleared more rapidly, the funds constituting the *float* were drawn down sooner, and the average amount of the customer's deposit thus declined.

4. In years when credit has been fairly readily available and competition in making loans has been strong, business borrowers have negotiated to reduce the size of their compensating balances, which has further lessened the rate of growth of demand deposits.

Banks began to realize that demand deposits had become like currency—the public will hold just so much and no more. With attractive interest rates now available from investments and savings institutions, the *opportunity cost,* or loss of income involved in leaving surplus funds in demand deposit form, is just too high for many individuals to accept. If individual banks and the banking system as a whole desire to grow as rapidly as the economy, they must turn to another fund source to supplement demand deposits.

This recognition of the general state of affairs, coupled with the competition from other institutions trying to lure the idle funds in individual depositors' accounts, made the banks do an about-face and realize that future bank growth depended at least as much on time and savings deposit solicitation as on demand deposit growth.

The Impact on Banking

The commercial banks started to solicit savings deposits from individuals by offering competitive interest rates on savings, and to solicit time deposits from corporations by beginning to offer them negotiable *time certificates of deposit* called CDs. These are deposits on which the principal and interest are paid at maturity to the bearer, rather than to a specific holder, so that a corporation can sell its CD to another investor if it needs its money back before the maturity date. As the banks became aggressive in the solicitation of time and savings deposits, the following developments occurred in the banking system.

Bank demand deposits were reduced, because unlike financial intermediaries, who place their funds into bank demand deposits, the commercial bank shows time and savings deposits as separate categories in the balance sheet, and does not deposit this money in demand deposits with itself or anyone else. Thus, when a depositor writes a check on his demand deposit to make a deposit in a commercial bank savings deposit or to buy a commercial bank time deposit, there is a reduction in bank demand deposits matching the rise in time and savings deposits.

However, since the Federal Reserve requires lower reserves to be maintained to back time and savings deposits than it requires to back demand deposits, a bank whose depositors have moved their money into time and savings deposit form can expand its lending and total deposits, even though the time and savings deposits came from its own demand deposit balances.

For example, if the Federal Reserve requires a 12-percent reserve to back demand deposits in a bank and a 4-percent reserve to back time and savings deposits, the movement of $100 from a demand to a savings account frees $8 of reserves held at the Federal Reserve. On the basis of this $8 of freed reserves, the bank itself may make only $8 of new loans and create that much in new deposits, unless it wishes to gamble on some of the deposits it is creating being redeposited with it by the recipients when the borrowers spend the money. However, since the banks need a 12-percent reserve behind demand deposits, and $8 of excess reserves have been created, the banking system as a whole will be able to create eight and one-third times as much as was freed when the required reserves were reduced, or $66.67 of new demand deposits; and if part of this newly created money is converted into time or savings deposits, the process can be repeated again with the reserves freed by this second conversion.

Thus, although the shift of money from a commercial bank to a financial intermediary results in no basic change in the size of demand deposits but rather leads to an increase in monetary velocity, solicitation of new savings and time deposits by a commercial bank does allow the creation of new bank deposits.

For the individual bank, then, the solicitation of time and savings deposits is a defensive competitive weapon against having customers' surplus demand deposit funds bid away to savings banks, savings and loan associations, and open-market investment instruments. To the banking system as a whole, it also allows more rapid growth, since the economy is financed more by expansion of bank deposits—albeit time and savings deposits—and less by increases in the velocity of turnover of money.

Whereas it is true that banks must pay interest on the time and savings deposits they generate and that this money formerly resided in demand deposits on which no interest payment was made, time and savings deposit solicitation is still a profitable venture for the bank.

First, the bank gets the deposit growth that follows when the deposits shift from demand to time and savings form and required reserves are reduced. This new deposit growth is, of course, matched by new interest-earning loans and investments.

Second, the slower growth of deposit velocity reduces bank costs of handling demand deposits.

Third, the banks are able to serve their borrowing and saving customers, and in doing so they get the other business that these customers provide. This is significant; if a bank turns down a customer either for a time deposit or a loan, it may lose that customer's entire business, or never gain this business if the customer is a good new prospect.

Finally, even though time and savings deposits cost interest whereas demand deposits do not, since they are considered to be more stable deposit funds for the bank, the bank can place them into longer-term, less liquid, and therefore higher-yielding loans and investments than those into which it can convert demand deposit funds. This is highly significant. The bank that uses its new savings funds aggressively can offset much of the cost of its interest payments, and the bank that makes its entire loan and investment portfolio more aggressive and higher yielding because it has a larger percentage of stable time and savings deposits on the liability side of its balance sheet may even more than offset the full cost of buying deposit funds that it used to get for free.

It must be said, though, that for most banks time and savings deposit growth is more expensive than demand deposit growth, but it is preferable, in terms of profitability and everything else, to the only realistic alternative available—no deposit growth at all.

The Impact on Monetary Controls

The changed attitude of the commercial banks toward the solicitation of time and savings deposits has played a significant role in reversing the decline of the role of banking in the economy. It has also had a valuable impact on the effectiveness of credit control.

The Federal Reserve's control mechanism is exercised through its control over the commercial banks. Therefore, if the banks' role in financing economic activity is reduced, it follows naturally that the Federal Reserve's controls are narrowed in overall impact too.

This does not mean that the Federal Reserve has lost any of its ability to limit spending in the economy to the levels it desires. The banking system's role in financing the economy may shrink, the growth in velocity of money that results as financial intermediaries grow taking up the slack, yet the Federal Reserve can still maintain the level of effective demand ($Money \times Velocity$ of money) at where it feels it should be.

The problem, however, is one of impact. To make an analogy, if a model of an automobile is made larger and larger but the brakes remain the same size, the only way to slow down this big car is to push harder on the braking mechanism that is available. Similarly, if the economy grows and the banking system does not grow as rapidly, the only control available to the Federal Reserve is to press down on the banking system harder and harder—by reducing the growth in bank reserves.

For the economy, the overall impact will be the same on spending whether the banks are restrained extra heavily to offset an increase in velocity or whether deposits grow more and velocity less; but to those borrowers in the economy dependent upon the commercial banks and not able to turn to other fund sources, placing more and more pressure on the commercial banks alone can be a seriously crippling force.

In the years when financial intermediaries became more and more important at the expense of the commercial banks, the money managers began to find themselves in the dilemma of having to allow monetary policy to decline in effectiveness or to restrict bank growth to a much greater extent than ever before, no matter how this hurt small business firms and other potential borrowers dependent upon bank loans with few, if any, alternative credit sources.[1]

[1]The issue is not really as black and white as we have pictured it, because there are ways in which tight money has an impact on financial intermediaries. For example, in a period of rising interest rates, savings banks and savings and loans cannot raise the yields they offer the public as rapidly as open-market interest rates rise, because their mortgages are long-maturity instruments. This means that the average income savings institutions receive on their mortgages does not rise rapidly, since only as new money comes in and mortgages mature can the savings institutions invest to gain the higher yields currently available. Thus the average income of savings institutions rises much more slowly than open-market interest rates do, and these institutions cannot raise the rates they pay savers fast enough to match the rise in yields available elsewhere.

The result is that in periods of tight money, individuals decide to channel their new flows of savings into higher-yielding market securities and even move money from savings institutions into open-market securities through a process called "disintermediation." As a result the savings banks and savings and loans have slower growth rates, which restricts their ability to lend.

The new attitude of the commercial banks in relying on time and savings deposits as a basic source of growth has lessened this problem, as the banks have become rapidly growing savings institutions and have regained their traditional share of the financing of the nation's credit needs. The threat to monetary policy's effectiveness that arose from the hesitancy of the banking business to compete for time and savings deposits has abated at least for the time being, and probably for good.

Ironically, though, the threat to the effectiveness of monetary policy that rose next stemmed from exactly the opposite corner, from over-aggressive banks. As banks began to solicit time and savings deposits to avoid loss of market share and a decreased role in the economy, some banks went much further and started to buy funds aggressively in order to purchase their way out of the effects of credit restraint. And although this aggressive liability-management policy could not offset the Federal Reserve's overall control over the total quantity of money and thus over the factor of M and V, it could and did bring serious new problems of distorted fund flows, marked interest-rate escalation, and subsequent economic decline, as the following chapter will indicate.

However, the impact of tight money on commercial banks is so much more direct than on savings banks, savings and loans, and other financial intermediaries that the Federal Reserve does face the dilemma of how to make credit control effective in a financial environment in which the commercial banks are growing more slowly than the economy without seriously hurting some bank borrowers. (A fuller discussion of the problems of thrift institutions can be found in Chapter 10.)

9

The Impact of Liability Management

The acceptance of the idea that commercial banking would have to buy deposit funds through the time and savings deposit route instead of merely relying on free checking-account deposits brought a major change in the industry.

In the past banks generally had felt that the size and rate of growth of their institutions depended upon the size and wealth of their territory, the number of their branches, and to some degree their aggressiveness in marketing. In sum, other than the modest impact that marketing could have, a bank felt that the territory it served would largely determine its size and activity.

But once banks accepted the concept of buying funds aggressively to avoid the loss of market share and of significance in financing the economy, it was a short step to the next concept of aggressively seeking funds for new lending and investing wherever they could be found, just so long as the loans and investments available were profitable enough to justify paying what the new funds cost in interest.

In sum, the buying of time and savings deposits made many bankers realize that they could be masters of their own fate with regard to size and importance, if they would only pay going interest rates for money on the market. Thus many bankers started to develop a variety of new ways in which money could be solicited —some of them cheaper than regular savings deposits and all of them supplements to solicitation of normal time and savings deposit funds for periods of heavy loan demands, when the available time and savings deposits of the community would not be adequate to meet all the solid loan requests on hand.

Prime among these new sources of funds has been the negotiable time certificate of deposit, or CD. Such certificates must be included in the category of new source of funds to supplement time and savings deposits, even though a CD is itself a time deposit because although banks had issued time deposits to local corporations before the early 1960s, the introduction of the negotiable time CD in 1961 provided them with a means of attracting funds from outside their own trading areas as well as from traditional customers. In effect, then, the CD allowed the bank to buy funds from investors everywhere who otherwise would have placed this money in the money market.

A second source of funds is the subordinated debenture. It is more expensive than the savings deposit on the basis of interest alone, but offers many advantages to offset the higher interest cost. Banks gaining debentures do not have to provide primary and secondary reserves behind them; they do not have to pay an assessment for them to the Federal Deposit Insurance Corporation for deposit insurance, as they had to for money in deposit form; they do not have the handling costs that savings deposits entail, since once the debenture is issued it remains on the bank's books, whereas savings deposits frequently flow in and out; and they do not have to back debentures with capital as they must back deposit growth, because a debenture is capital and does not need capital backing, as a deposit does.

Thus, through the sale of subordinated capital debentures, some banks started to tap the organized capital market for funds to meet growing loan demands, even though most debenture issuers still use the medium only to supply inexpensive capital to cushion deposit growth.

Finally, banks also started to turn to the federal funds market as a source of funds. Originally the federal funds market was an informal structure by which banks that were short of reserves at the Federal Reserve Bank of their district could borrow the excess reserves held at Federal by other banks. This did not hurt credit control but rather helped it. The Federal Reserve concerns itself with the overall picture of credit availability, and so if one bank has excess reserves at a time when the Federal Reserve wants to tighten credit, the Federal Reserve authorities are happy to have these reserves lent to another bank, because then it knows that more of the reserves it has made available have been utilized. This is valuable to the Federal Reserve, since otherwise it has only one alternative: to ignore the fact that some reserves are unused, and thus allow the economy's utilized reserves to be below what the economy can absorb in spending, or to compensate for these idle reserves by allowing new reserves to be created, so as to bring the spending level to the point it wants. However, if the Federal Reserve takes the latter course, there is always the possibility that the bank with the excess reserves will start using them, with the result that too much credit will become available in the economy. The Federal Reserve prefers a taut money market, with all available reserves being used, so that its control is exact, and since the federal funds market helps make such taut conditions in the money market, it helps rather than hinders credit policy implementation.

Banks, then, first looked at the federal funds market solely as a means of obtaining reserves from other banks when a deficiency in their own reserve positions developed. This kept the federal funds borrowing rate at or below the Federal Reserve's own discount rate, because banks always knew that if they needed reserves to meet a temporary deficiency and the federal funds rate exceeded the discount rate, they could borrow from the Federal Reserve and save the additional interest cost.

Then it was recognized that the federal funds of other banks might well serve as a cheap source of lendable funds as well as a means of meeting reserve deficiencies. First, banks started borrowing other banks' federal funds at rates up to the discount rate, not just to meet reserve deficiencies, but also to lend this money for profit. Then the banks realized that when federal funds were scarce it was worthwhile paying even more than the discount rate for federal funds held by other banks, if the loans to be made with this money offered an even higher rate than the federal funds cost. (A bank would not, of course, go to the Federal Reserve discount window to borrow money in order to lend it out in new loans, since this is not a legitimate use of the discount privilege. The discount rate, therefore, served as a ceiling for federal funds rates when the sole purpose of borrowing was to meet reserve deficiencies, a purpose for which borrowing from Federal is legal; but when the money was used to make new loans, then the discount window no longer was a possible alternative source of funds and it ceased to be a ceiling on the rates federal funds would trade at.)

Thus, banks found three new sources of funds that would bring in money from all over the nation: time CDs, debentures, and federal funds. With the knowledge that new money could be bought when wanted if the bank were willing and able to pay enough for it, another basic change occurred in banking. The banks that felt they could always attract as much money as they needed by paying enough for it started to reduce their secondary reserve positions. They felt that keeping money liquid is expensive, and rather than keep a lot of money tied up in low-yielding but liquid loans and investments, they could place it out into higher-yielding longer-term loans and buy liquidity when it was needed through the sale of CDs or the purchase of federal funds. (Debentures were not used for such short-term purposes, since they take a long time to plan and sell and are generally of about twenty years' maturity.)

Certainly the purchase of liquidity could be expensive, especially when other banks were trying to buy liquidity at the same time, but it was far less expensive than sacrificing income, year after year, income possessing excess liquidity waiting until it might be needed.

From this evolved the next step aggressive bankers began to adopt, the management of the bank's liabilities, instead of concentrating on asset management, as a way of adjusting the bank balance sheet to changed conditions.

Goals of Liability Management

As Chapter Five attempted to show, the traditional bank approach to the obtaining and allocation of funds has made the liability, or source of funds, side of the balance sheet fairly passive while it has made the asset, or uses of funds sector, the one receiving the banker's attention.

The banker felt, "My deposits are controlled by the wealth of my community and its ability to keep funds in the bank, so the real area in which I can exercise some control is in the type of assets I convert my deposit funds into." Therefore the deposit side of the balance sheet received little active attention, and the banker devoted himself to earning the best possible return compatible with safety and liquidity that he could gain from lending and investing his deposit funds and stockholders' capital.

The trends toward first buying time and savings deposits and then buying liquidity has made some bankers recognize, however, that in the competitive economy in which we live and with the changes that have taken place in the sources of bank funds, it may well be that now the banker often has more control over the liability side of his balance sheet than he has over his assets.

Although it is all well and good for the banker to say that he will schedule the types of loans and loan maturities that match the stability of his deposit funds, in a competitive economy this is not always possible. A banker can decide that he will have a certain percentage of short-term loans on his books, because a certain percentage of his deposits have high volatility; but deciding that this is what he wants is one matter, and obtaining this type of loan may be another entirely. If the community wants longer-term loans for major capital projects and the banker insists on short-term self-liquidating loans of the type used to finance seasonal inventory purchases, if he is in a competitive environment the banker will soon find himself with few loans on the book and a consequent erosion in his deposit and profit picture.

Through aggressive promotion and by changing standards to adjust to the credit standing of the borrowers who want the maturity and type of loan he desires to make, a banker can do something to encourage the types of loans he wants; but basically, when the economy is competitive and is not operating near capacity, the borrower is in the driver's seat, and the banker either makes the type of loan the borrower wants or makes no loan at all. The asset side of the bank balance sheet is much less under the control of the banker than was the case when credit was not available from alternative sources and the banker could more or less dictate his terms in lending.

Conversely, at the same time as it has become harder and harder for the banker to manage his asset portfolio, because some banks can now buy more of their liabilities and can buy them from all over the nation, they have much more control over their liabilities, or sources of funds, than ever before. If his bank has need of more funds, the banker merely raises the rate he pays for savings, time deposits, CDs, federal funds, and, if his loan demands seem of long-term duration, even debentures.

A direct about-face has occurred. Whereas in the past the banker accepted his liabilities and managed his assets to fit his liability posture, now many bankers have accepted the fact that asset portfolios, and loans in particular, are dictated by the market, and to a greater degree the bank's liability structure can be managed to match the loan demands that the bank has available.

On the surface this seems like a simple shift in bank operations of little significance to the rest of the economy, but it has brought and is bringing a basic change in the financial structure and in the impact of the Federal Reserve's monetary policy.

Understanding the structural impact of liability management involves recalling the fact that funds can be channeled from savers to investors in several ways: The money can flow directly; it can move into and out of the organized money and capital markets; it can flow into financial intermediaries and then into the organized money and capital markets; or it can flow into the organized money and capital markets and thence into the hands of financial intermediaries for lending out. In all this, the commercial banks have played a combined role of financial intermediaries —lending what they receive—and the basic institutional force involved in the creation of new money, when the money they have received has resulted from the availability of new reserves and has not just been a shift from one bank's demand deposits to another's.

Yet in their role as financial intermediaries the banks have acted as the savings banks and savings and loan associations act, serving as middlemen between the public's savings and the loans and investments available in direct lending and in the organized money and capital market.

Now, however, through liability management, some commercial banks have added another function to their economic role in the circular flow of funds. When they find they do not obtain enough funds from direct deposits to meet loan demands, they have started drawing on the organized money and capital markets for funds—through federal funds, CDs, and the subordinated capital debenture. The result of this is that these banks have made themselves into another link between the organized money and capital markets and the economy, drawing in funds that formerly went into traditional money and capital market instruments, such as government securities and corporate and municipal bonds, and placing them instead in the variety of loans and investments that banks make.

To the economy, of course, this means a more effective flow of funds through the intermediation process; by tapping the organized money and capital markets these banks have intensified the competition for available investment funds in those markets, which in turn has meant a more efficient allocation of available funds to those uses which offer the lender the best return compatible with the risk he is willing to take.

Thus, these banks have become part of a two-way pump for funds in the circular flow-of-funds process. They pump funds from the depositors either to the borrowers of the nation who want individual loans or to the borrowers who are large enough to utilize the organized money and capital markets, moving the funds where the return is greatest. Moreover, now they also pump funds that others have placed in the organized money and capital markets out of these impersonal markets and into the lending opportunities that they themselves have generated.

Any intermediation process can occur only when the mover of funds finds opportunities to profit from the spread between buying and selling rates, and since the commercial banks' entrance into both markets narrows the spreads between rates, the new activities of these banks help to even out interest rate differentials in the economy. They also channel funds to where they are evidently needed most, since they are rewarded there with the highest return.

Impact on Credit Control

While the commercial banks' new role of financial intermediaries between the organized money and capital markets and the individual borrowers of the economy makes the flow of funds more efficient, it has a decided influence on the effectiveness of credit control.

This influence takes place not through a lessening of the overall effectiveness of the credit control mechanism but rather through an alteration in the areas of its impact, which in its own right can be a disturbing factor to the Federal Reserve.

At first, one might feel that the banks' ability to obtain new funds from the money and capital markets would enable the banking system to escape from the impact of credit control. Certainly the banks that sell debentures and issue CDs are obtaining new funds that can be lent. Yet, just as when the Federal Reserve is maintaining stable reserve levels a bank cannot get a deposit without having some other bank lose this deposit; when a bank sells debentures of CDs the money it receives must come from somewhere. Except in the improbable event that the money comes from cash hoards, it must come from the debenture buyers or from the CD buyers' demand deposit.

It is true that if money flows from demand deposits into CDs there is a reduction in reserve requirements, which allows banks to create new loans and thus expand deposit levels. If money flows from demand deposits into debentures, even more expansionary power is given the bank because, whereas the demand deposit requires a high reserve backing and the time deposit a lower backing, the debenture—not being a deposit—requires no backing. Thus, the full amount flowing from demand deposits into debentures is freed from reserve requirements, and the commercial banks gain that much of an increase in excess reserves.

But this does not rob the Federal Reserve of its effectiveness. If reserves are freed by the shift of funds from demand to time or savings deposits, or even by the shift of funds from demand deposits to debentures, the Federal Reserve can offset this freeing of reserves simply by tightening up its own open market operations to the same extent.

However, the change in banking from asset allocation to liability management does affect the impact credit control has on differing sectors of the banking system.

The bank that is able to sell CDs or debentures or to buy federal funds can thereby attract new money to meet liquidity needs or new loan demands. In so doing it can obtain the funds it desires, whether or not the Federal Reserve is attempting to maintain tight money. To the banking system at large, Federal Reserve credit restraint means less money to lend, but to the banks able to buy growth, there is business as usual and a declining influence of the Federal Reserve.

Of course, what must be recognized is that the money these

banks are able to obtain in tight money periods must come from somewhere, and "somewhere" is banks that are not able to compete on a rate basis and therefore cannot keep funds from being drawn into other institutions. The banks that make themselves immune to the impact of credit control do so by drawing in funds from other banks, and thereby make these other institutions doubly susceptible to the impact of tight money.

Traditionally, the Federal Reserve has followed quantitative credit controls, setting the reserve levels and letting the impact of this tightness fall where it may. In this regard it has been like a zoo keeper who has twenty-four fish to throw to three seals each day and does not care whether each seal gets eight fish or whether one gets twenty-four and the other two starve, just so long as twenty-four fish, no more and no less, are consumed.

Under this policy, the banks whose loan demands had been strong and profitable enough for them to pay high rates for money and whose stature in the money and capital markets was such as to draw to them the funds they wanted had been making themselves immune to a degree to the impact of credit control. Since the weaker and smaller banks, the savings banks, and savings and loans had been bearing the brunt of credit control's tightening pressure, to offset this the Federal Reserve took some measures to make credit control more qualitative in nature and direct in its impact.

In the summer of 1966, the Federal Reserve started utilizing its control over the banks' time and savings deposit interest rates, making it a basic weapon of credit control to supplement traditional monetary policy weapons in a period of extremely tight money. This involved keeping the interest ceilings under the Federal Reserve's Regulation Q so low that these aggressive banks could not legally continue to pay enough interest on time and savings deposits to buy all the funds they wanted, even if they could afford to do so. They could no longer buy their way out of bearing a share of the impact of credit control.

The Federal Reserve had as its aim the hobbling of the liability-management practice of the major banks so that the smaller banks and the nonbank financial intermediaries could get more of the available funds in a tight money period. But matters did not work out that way.

The aggressive banks could not compete for the time and savings funds of the nation in 1966, and again in 1969, because they were limited in what they could pay in interest on these deposits by Regulation Q; but open-market interest rates in the nation soared to their highest levels since the 1860s. The savers, therefore, instead of having their money sit in smaller banks, savings banks, and savings and loan associations, and thus earning the lower interest that these institutions could afford to pay, took much of the money away from the financial institutions entirely and placed it directly into open-market securities, such as short-term U.S. Treasury bills and commercial paper issued by nonfinancial corporations and finance companies for the purpose of tapping the savings of the nation. This process was termed *disintermediation,* because it involved the direct placement of the public's funds into money market instruments without channeling them first through banks or financial intermediaries.

The lesson to the money managers was clear: If they hobbled the aggressive institutions by limiting what they could pay for funds and thus prevented them from receiving the lion's share of available money in a tight money period, they were also hobbling the public by preventing it from earning the higher time and savings deposit interest rates that these aggressive banks were willing to pay.

Instead of aiding the smaller banks, the weaker banks, and the savings banks and savings and loan associations, the Federal Reserve's Regulation Q was penalizing all the financial institutions by inducing the public to bypass them.

The Federal Reserve found it impossible to alter its policy during the tight money period of 1969 because of a fear that a relaxation of Regulation Q would lead to an interest rate competition among institutions for funds, which could cause even more damage to the poorer earners.

Yet commercial banks could not sit idly by and watch their lifeblood disappear. Although it is true that money that leaves bank time and savings deposits and goes directly into money market instruments will come back into the banking system as the demand deposits of the institution that borrowed in the money market, the banks were still hurt. Because in the same way that banks gained new free reserves and the ability to create more deposit money when they started fighting for time and savings deposits, as indicated in Chapter Eight (because demand deposits shifted into time and savings deposit form on which lower reserves must be maintained), disintermediation led to the exact opposite.

What occurred then is that, as people took time deposit funds and savings deposit money and placed them directly into open market securities, the money came back as demand deposits of the open-market borrower. But the banks faced a serious squeeze on their reserves for two reasons.

First, the bank losing the time or savings deposit would not necessarily be the one to receive the demand deposit.

Second, the demand deposits required a higher percentage of reserve backing than did the time and savings deposits. And in the tight money periods of 1966 and 1969, the banks did not have the free reserves available to meet these higher reserve requirements. Thus, as disintermediation developed, they were forced to sell investments at the low prices then in effect, not to renew loans, and to curb lending activity even more in order to get deposits down, and reserves up, to the levels mandated by the higher reserve requirements.

The result was that major banks took two drastic steps to get around this reserve squeeze and the hobbles of Regulation Q.

First, they started to look to their offshore offices as a source of more and more Eurodollar funds—the dollars owned by foreign individuals and institutions that could be attracted into deposits in offshore offices of American banks by attractive interest rates and then brought home into the banks in need of reserves.

Because the Federal Reserve cannot control what an American bank pays for deposits obtained in Nassau or on the continent of Europe, major American banks bid as much as 13 percent for short-term dollar deposits in these offshore offices to meet the reserve deficiencies at home caused by disintermediation.

What they actually received when they paid as much as 13 percent for a dollar deposit in an offshore office (that is, a Eurodollar deposit) was a check or other claim on some American bank, because this is the only form in which dollars can be obtained (other than through the deposit of cash).[1] But the individual banks that bought Eurodollars did get the dollars they needed for their reserve positions, even if other U.S. banks lost these dollars of reserves. And because Eurodollar funds transferred from offshore offices to the American office of an American bank were then not considered to be deposits and thus were not subject to reserve requirements, the banks found Eurodollars to be that much more attractive as a source of funds to meet reserve deficiencies. Because unlike deposit inflows, of which one-sixth or so of the funds obtained have to be idled as required reserves, all the inflow from Eurodollar deposits could be utilized to help meet the reserve squeeze that disintermediation had caused.

Second, in the late 1960s and the beginning of the 1970s, banks representing over 40 percent of the entire American industry's assets converted from their status as banks into one-bank holding company form, as another way of gaining new fund sources not subject to Regulation Q or to reserve requirements.

The banks saw that finance companies and other institutions could borrow on the open market, pay as much as the traffic would require, and not have to idle any of the receipts in sterile reserves at the Federal Reserve. And noting that, owing to a loophole in the law, authorities did not regulate holding companies that owned only one bank, many of these banking institutions arranged to convert their shareholders' property from control of a bank to control of a holding company that then owned the one bank. To the shareholder it made little difference whether he owned the stock of a bank or the stock of a company whose sole asset was the stock of the bank. But to the bank's operation it made a drastic

---

[1] What the Eurodollar shows is that, except for cash, money never leaves the country of origin, only the ownership does. When foreigners earn dollars, these dollars remain as deposits in American banks, and only the ownership transfers abroad. Even if the holders of these dollars buy Eurodollars, all they do is add an extra step of transferring their dollar deposit in the United States to the Eurodollar soliciting bank, while they get a claim on that offshore bank instead. And if the offshore bank makes a loan with the Eurodollar proceeds, it gives the borrower its check or draft on the deposit in the United States it obtained when it purchased the Eurodollar. The development of the Eurodollar market thus does not bring new money into the United States and it does not create new U.S. dollars. All it does is turn present dollars over faster, and in this way it works like any other financial intermediary, speeding up the velocity of money.

difference. Because, whereas the bank was subject to reserve requirements and Regulation Q, the parent holding company was just another nonbank corporation, and as such was no more subject to bank restraints than would be a railroad, a finance company, or any other company borrowing in the open market.

Thus these one-bank holding companies sold their own commercial paper to the investors who were practicing disintermediation, and so were able to pay going rates for the funds, ignore reserve requirements, and then participate as co-lenders with the subsidiary bank in the making of new loans, as a way of utilizing these funds to serve bank customers.

In addition, because the holding companies owned only one bank and therefore were not subject to control by the banking authorities as the law was then constituted, they could also undertake nonbank operations ranging from the leasing of equipment and the handling of data processing for customers, on to the limitless range of activities that any American corporation can undertake if it is not subject to the special restraints imposed on commercial banks to protect the funds of their depositors.

Thus the Federal Reserve's Regulation Q had created a monster. Major banks were gaining more and more of their funds from outside the nation, and almost half the assets of the industry had converted into the one-bank holding company form to get around Federal Reserve restraints on growth and variety of services that could be offered.

The Federal Reserve had to alter this situation, and it did. Obviously, the Federal Reserve's first step was to subject the Eurodollar and commercial paper fund sources of the banks to reserve requirements. Otherwise, before too long, the entire industry would have undertaken the practice of obtaining funds through these nondeposit sources, which in turn would have lessened substantially the Federal Reserve's credit control powers.

As for Regulation Q, fate played an interesting trick in downgrading its importance; when the Penn Central Transportation Company failed in 1970 and the holders of that company's commercial paper found they now held an illiquid asset of dubious value, many investors got scared. They recognized that the commercial paper they were buying in order to get a higher yield than the banks could pay under Regulation Q was not the riskless substitute for bank CDs they had thought it to be. And as these investors stopped buying new commercial paper, the companies that had sold this paper, and counted on selling more to refinance maturing obligations, faced a serious liquidity squeeze.

Naturally these companies in need of funds to pay off maturing commercial paper came back to the banks when paper buyers disappeared because they had no alternative fund source. But the Regulation Q hobble prevented the banks from obtaining the funds that these other potential borrowers desperately needed to meet liquidity squeezes, so the companies had to be turned away empty-handed. Thus far more commercial paper than just that of the Penn Central might have defaulted if the Federal Reserve had finally not given in and relaxed the ceiling of Regulation Q on deposits of $100,000 and over to allow the banks to get enough new CD money to meet the needs of these companies with maturing paper to pay off.

What the Federal Reserve apparently recognized is that the nation needs bank credit as the reliable backstop for emergencies. And when it so hobbles the banks that they cannot obtain the funds needed for lending the financial structure of the nation is weakened.

But, as we also learned, excessive easing of restraint weakens the financial structure. The relaxing of the Regulation Q ceiling on large sized deposits so freed the major banks from their hobbles that we witnessed the most aggressive liability management seen so far. And this in turn set the stage for the credit crunch of 1973–1974 and helped bring the recession following that period.

Once the banks were freed from the interest ceiling on large CDs, many became certain that they could meet any profitable loan demand that came along. They felt they would never again be caught short of lendable funds if they were only willing to pay market rates for money.

Thus banks made long-term loans that they counted on funding by rolling over and over short-term Eurodollars, holding company commercial paper, and especially negotiable CDs. Since long-term loans generally yield more than money market funds cost, these banks felt this would be a profitable approach. And if, for short time periods, costs of money market funds did rise to exceed what the long-term loans earned, most of the time the situation would be the other way around, making the venture profitable on balance. On top of this, by providing long-term loans and long-term commitments to their good customers, the banks felt they were doing their good business customers a favor by immunizing them from the effects of tight money, since these banks and their customers would always obtain the funds they needed, and others would end up the sufferers from Federal Reserve credit restraint.

This approach, however, left the aggressive banks with a tiger by the tail. For no matter how expensive short-term funds became, the banks had to renew maturing money market instruments, since the funds had already been lent and the banks thus could not repay short-term obligations as they matured.

This placed the Fed in a dilemma. If the Fed sat back and let the banks bid rates higher and higher to renew successively maturing money market paper, it would be blamed for letting credit costs get too high. But if the Fed provided new reserves to help the banks obtain some of the funds needed, it would be blamed for allowing an inflationary increase in the money supply.

The Fed did allow some money supply expansion, although basically it had no choice but to let the banks bid money market rates up to levels not witnessed since the Civil War. The record interest rates, exemplified by a 12-percent prime rate, brought trouble to many borrowers whose rates were tied to prime rather than fixed in advance. Notable among these were real estate financiers, who found it impossible to complete their projects profitably with money costing as much as 18 percent a year. Many defaulted, hurting thereby both the banks and the Real Estate Investment Trusts (REIT) that had financed their operations. And since many of these REITs in turn were utilizing bank financing, the banks were doubly hurt as both their real estate construction loans and their REIT loans went into default.

Because of a number of forces, including the oil embargo, the rise in the price of energy, and other factors, but also in large part because of the tight money and credit collapse that bank liability management had caused, the economy then entered the worst recession since the Great Depression of the 1930s. And with the recession came a new era of conservatism for both the banks and the Fed.

The banks found that the high interest rates which they helped to cause led to loan defaults by many interest-rate-sensitive borrowers. And ironically, many of the large corporations that the banks had tried to immunize from credit restraint through their liability-management policies showed no particular loyalty either —many paid off their loans and moved to cheaper money market fund sources as soon as the economy slumped and interest rates fell, even though the banks by then badly needed these loans on their books.

What bothered the Fed was that large banks had been protecting their large customers from the impact of credit restraint, with other potential borrowers—notably home buyers, state and local governments, and smaller and new businesses—as the main sufferers.

The Federal Reserve is thus likely to interfere to a greater extent if banks do decide to turn to aggressive liability management again. It is likely that the Fed would use its "open mouth policy" of moral suasion, exhortations, and threats to keep banks from turning again to intense usage of a borrowing-short, lending-long policy. In doing so, the Fed's power over member bank capital adequacy requirements and its powers to decide whether member bank branches should be allowed or whether holding company acquisitions should be approved certainly will be relied upon to induce less aggressive behavior.

As for the banks themselves, many have turned from the experiment with unbridled liability management to a newer approach of asset/liability management, a far more balanced approach. And young lending officers who felt that loans could never go sour have learned otherwise.

The experiment with liability management means therefore that we are seeing more regulatory intervention in bank lending, investing, and deposit solicitation policy than ever before, whether by formal or informal methods. Thus the recent experiment with liability management has changed the face of commercial banking.

Yet what may have been changing bank operations and policies even more radically has been the growing expansion of the powers of savings banks, of savings and loan associations, of credit unions, and of other nonbank financial institutions and the need for the commercial banks to respond to this growing competitive threat.

It is to a discussion of why the thrifts have been changing and what this means for commercial banking that we must turn next.

10

The Changing Role of the Thrifts

As each day passes, it becomes harder and harder to differentiate among financial institutions in the United States.

The savings banks, savings and loans, and credit unions are steadily obtaining more and more powers to offer services—powers that formerly were the exclusive province of the commercial banking industry. And, as a result, the competitive environment that bankers face is becoming steadily more severe.

What is ironic is that not only have the thrifts obtained powers to offer these broader services, but in their efforts to diversify, the thrifts have also forced radical changes on banking blessed by some bankers and damned by others. Looking at the changes in banking on the horizon—interest on demand deposits, remote banking through point of sale terminals, and the general popularization of electronic funds-transfer services as the means of delivering banking service—one cannot forget that virtually all these changes were inaugurated by the thrift institutions rather than the banks themselves. The commercial banks have instead been in a reactive mode—accepting the changes imposed on the way banking services are delivered by the innovative thrifts.

And what makes many bankers so mad at themselves is that much of this competition could have been avoided, and the control over change could have remained in the hands of the bankers themselves if the industry had only taken a positive attitude toward change in the years immediately following World War II.

Yet, in accordance with the Biblical prophecy that the sins of the fathers shall be visited upon the third generation, we see bankers today paying the price for negative banking practices of two and three decades ago. The only positive feature, however, is that acute bankers today have been able to see the bright side of these changes and to make the most of the opportunities inherent in them while minimizing the disadvantages through careful cost analysis, marketing studies, and reevaluation of the goals of the bank to emphasize what is profitable.

The Background

It is impossible to evaluate the goals and operations of the thrift industry without remembering that in the years immediately following World War II all too many commercial bankers lived by the motto "Never do something the first time." The world was their oyster, and they felt no need to compromise in any way to meet changing public needs. After all, interest rates were so low that corporations and individual depositors were willing to leave money in demand deposit form out of sheer absence of profitable alternatives.

The banking industry had seen no reason to stress the solicitation of time and savings deposits, because free demand deposits provided an adequate supply of funds. And many bankers also felt that the industry should concentrate on commercial lending rather than build portfolios of home mortgages.

The result was, however, a void in the availability of financial services that the thrift institutions were ready, willing, and able to fill. With the banks de-emphasizing savings deposits and mortgages, the thrifts had a natural vacuum that they could fill in the solicitation of funds and in their use.

As some have put it, the thrifts practiced the rule of 3, 6, and 3. "We'll take your money at 3 percent, we'll lend it back to you at 6, and we will be on the golf course by 3." These were the halcyon days of the thrifts and they grew larger and more and more prosperous, filling the void that the commercial banks had left for them.

The 1960s

But conditions changed in the 1960s. After the thrifts had grown from infants to giant competitors, the commercial banking industry finally decided to enter the fray and win back the business it had lost by default. As we have seen, there were basic reasons for this course from the bankers' viewpoint.

First, interest rates had been rising, so that the banks found they could no longer count on obtaining the volumes of demand deposit funds they formerly had obtained. Rather, corporate and municipal treasurers found it more advantageous to place surplus funds into Treasury bills and other money market instruments rather than leave the money idle in checking account balances. The banks finally were forced to offer negotiable time certificates of deposit to win back some of the money that corporate treasurers, municipal officials, and others were pulling from banks and placing into open-market securities.

A similar situation was developing with regard to individual balances. People were taking money from checking accounts and placing it into time and savings deposits at the thrifts to take advantage of the higher rates the thrifts were offering and the aggressive promotion they had undertaken to obtain funds.

As discussed above, the total sum of money in the economy would not change if this money were to flow into money market instruments and savings deposits instead of into bank demand balances; the recipients of the money—be they the vendors who sold goods to the Treasury or the borrowers of funds from the thrifts or the thrifts themselves—had to place it back into demand balances. This is where money resides.

But by not competing for funds, the banks saw that the money supply remained fairly static, with economic activity financed by augmented velocity of the same money supply. Moreover, each individual bank that desired to insure its own growth had to compete aggressively to insure its share of the available deposits.

In sum, the farsighted commercial bankers determined that time and savings deposits were much more expensive than demand deposits, but far preferable to the real alternative available —no deposits.

The banks then began to compete aggressively for time and savings funds. And immediately the thrifts began to realize that in a free market they were at a basic disadvantage against the commercial banks in competing for the public's savings. The commercial banks had short-term assets that could be rolled over at times of rising interest rates, so that yields the banks could earn and could pay would rise as general interest rates rose.

But since the thrifts were locked in with long-term mortgages as the backbone of their asset structures, they could not turn their assets over to get the new higher yields, at least for the ten to twenty years until their mortgages matured. Thus they could not afford to pay rates as high as the banks could pay for new savings. They also feared that they would lose to the commercials some of the savings they already had, once the banks began aggressive competition for time and savings funds.

Faced with a profits squeeze, the possible loss of savings on hand, and even the possibility of forced liquidation of mortgages at a loss to meet the outflow of funds that might develop as banks paid higher rates than the thrifts could afford, the savings banks and savings and loans recognized that they could no longer regard the marketplace as an advantageous arena in which to compete. No wonder they turned to Washington for help.

The Restraints

What the thrift industry desired, and got, was protection from competition and competitive rates. The Federal Reserve Board's Regulation Q was utilized to insure that the commercial banks would not only be prevented from paying as much as they could afford to pay for time and savings deposits, but also that they were prevented from paying as much as the thrifts were allowed to offer the public.

This so-called "differential" became the savior of the thrifts for a good while. And it is still defended heatedly by most of the thrift industry. Because it means that the savings banks, savings and loans, and the commercial banks for that matter, that cannot or do not want to pay top dollar for savings would be protected from a serious outflow of funds to the aggressive commercial banks that can afford to pay more for savings and are anxious to use this rate weapon to draw in funds from less profitable and less aggressive financial institutions.

But there was a good reason why many commercial banks had to take definite action in response to the Federal Reserve's Regulation Q ceiling and the differential. For many commercial banks had switched from asset allocation over to aggressive liability management.

Asset allocation had involved obtaining funds, analyzing the volatility of this money, and then lending and investing to match the loans and investment maturities to the length of time the bank felt it would be able to keep its deposits.

But this was an essentially passive approach to loans and investments, because their maturity and volume depended on whatever types of funds the bank was able to obtain on the liability side. As we have seen, aggressive banks decided in the mid-1960s to turn this around and make the assets the basic determinant of bank policy. Thus they started to make every loan and sound investment they felt would be profitable and then funded these assets with money purchased through time and savings deposit solicitation.

The approach involved the recognition that if a bank does not accommodate its borrowing customers with the volumes of funds they want and with the maturity structure they desire, the bank will not be able to cement relationships and grow. But it also involved making absolutely certain that the bank could buy the funds it needed through aggressive solicitation of time and savings deposits. If it made the loans and then went out to find the money, it had to be certain the money sources would not dry up —leaving the bank with a serious liquidity squeeze.

Yet the new Regulation Q ceilings made this very fear of the bankers into a day-to-day occurrence. If they could not pay going rates for time and savings deposits under the Regulation Q ceilings, then they could have no assurance that they could obtain the money they needed. Because when rates on other vehicles in the money market were higher than banks were allowed to pay, the fund sources that the banks so counted upon would immediately dry up. Thus banks started to develop means of getting around Regulation Q through new techniques and organizational changes, notably the use of the Eurodollar and of commercial paper issued by bank holding companies.

But what most worried the thrift institutions was not this use of the Eurodollar and the holding company's borrowing power as a way around Regulation Q; this only attracted large sums that would normally flow into large denomination certificates of deposit that the thrifts did not solicit. Rather, it was the continued drain of small-sized savings deposits from the thrifts even after they had the blanket of protection provided by Regulation Q. For what developed was disintermediation.

Disintermediation

Disintermediation, it will be recalled, involves simply moving funds from the savings deposits of individuals, charities, and others, and placing this money directly into the money market to take advantage of opportunities when money market rates are above those the thrifts and banks are allowed to offer under the Regulation Q ceiling.

As open-market interest rates rose, many individuals learned that they could do far better buying Treasury bills and other money market securities than they could holding money in saving accounts.

Furthermore, taking advantage of the hobbles that Regulation Q placed on commercial banks and thrifts in the competition for the funds of the saver, new institutions developed that were willing to accept smaller denomination savings and to pay rates much closer to going-money-market levels for this money than the banks and the thrifts were allowed to offer under the Federal Reserve's ceilings.

At first it was merely entrepreneurs who would put packages of $1,000 together to make $10,000 bundles for investment in Treasury bills, when the Treasury tried to help the thrifts avoid disintermediation by raising the minimum amount needed for investment in Treasury bills from $1,000 to the $10,000 level.

But later the real threat developed through the inauguration of money market mutual funds and then municipal bond mutual funds, whose aim was to attract funds that formerly flowed into savings deposits, with the lure being the higher rates that were available in money market instruments but which the thrifts and the banks were prohibited from paying because of Regulation Q's ceiling.

Thus forward-thinking thrift executives finally realized that the future of their industry did not depend so much upon restricting their competitiors. Rather, it depended upon gaining more powers for themselves, both on the asset side and the liability side. And as they evaluated where their industry was going, they also had a chance to look at some other fundamental changes in the habits of the American people that made a diversification of thrift powers a must, if their industry were to survive.

As the thrift leaders began to examine what was happening to American financial habits, they learned the following facts about savers that scared many of them into understanding that traditional policies, if continued, would be a dead-end street.

Saving for a rainy day was being deemphasized. Savings institutions had always advertised and promoted the fact that a savings account was the basic bastion of the individual against financial insecurity. People should "save for a rainy day."

But what the thrifts began to learn was that in the 1960s and 1970s, this motive for saving had dropped sharply in the public's minds. For one thing the cost of illness had become so overwhelming that most people felt they could cover it only with medical insurance rather than their own savings. And with regard to retirement funds, education money, and other needs for which savings had been amassed in the past, people saw the government taking over more of the role that individuals used to have.

All too often we have heard stories of the family that saved $5,000 or $10,000 for a child's education, only to find that now the family had too much money for the child to be eligible for a scholarship and not enough to pay the tuition. If the family had saved nothing, the child would have been better off, since he or she would have been eligible for a scholarship. In sum, saving for a rainy day had been a poor decision.

Saving to "make a buck" has been hurt by inflation. It is hard for the public to accept the idea that a savings account is a good use of funds when inflation expands at a faster rate than interest on savings is earned (even forgetting the fact that the interest on savings is then subject to income taxes). As a result many people have begun to take the attitude that it is silly to save, and that they are far better off spending their money while they can, before it loses even more of its value. Unless inflation decreases far more than most economists expect it will, this difficulty in motivating people to save will remain.

People want "one stop banking." Leading thrift executives have also recognized that the thrift industry must offer the convenience of one-stop banking or it will lose out to commercial banks, even with a modest ¼ percent Regulation Q differential—which appears to be the size of the differential that Congress will accept for the foreseeable future.

If the thrifts only take savings deposits and make mortgage loans, they will slowly and steadily lose out to the full-service commercial bank. Thus they feel they must diversify for this reason too.

The age of the saver is rising. Americans generally do not save until they get older; younger people are far more likely to be in debt. Thus if the thrifts do not want to be categorized as the institution of the aged, they must develop other means of attracting deposits than merely concentrating on savings and time deposits.

Savings deposits cost more than other sources of funds. On top of all this, the thrifts look at the high cost of savings deposits, and especially the higher cost of the longer-term time certificates of deposits that they had to start to solicit to solve the "borrowing short, lending long" dilemma, and they get scared. They see that their cost of funds is extremely high, and if mortgage rates do fall, they will be locked in with high-cost time certificates in the face of slackening yield levels.

In sum, thrifts face the irony that they started to develop longer-term certificates of deposit to solve the dilemma of borrowing short and lending long in an environment of rising interest rates. And yet, because they have borrowed long, they fear that if interest rates do move down and they are locked in with their long-term certificates, they may suffer the exact opposite squeeze of having borrowed long while their mortgage loans roll over to be refinanced at lower yields—making them the victims of a policy of borrowing long and having to lend short.

Thus the thrifts feel they need a number of basic changes in their powers if they are to survive, and they are fighting to obtain them.

What Do the Thrifts Want?

First and foremost, they want the continuation of the Regulation Q differential while they alter their powers. And many want it to remain in effect permanently. For they feel that in a "hands off" fight, the commercial banks could beat the thrifts badly, and they do not want to see the banks able to use their convenience advantage, earnings advantage, and the muscle they feel the banks gain from the exclusive serving of corporate business to beat down the thrifts.

But at the same time as the thrifts want the banks to be subject to the hobbles of the Regulation Q differential, many thrift executives want more and more bank powers themselves. They definitely desire checking account power; they feel that such power will solve a number of their problems. It will help provide a new service to savers who are unhappy with saving for a rainy day, who feel that interest on savings is not worthwhile saving for today in an era of high inflation. The account will also provide a service for the young who do not save much. They also feel that obtaining checking accounts will lessen the need to rely so greatly on time certificates of deposit and will thus lessen the earnings squeeze that now comes from the need to pay the higher rates that certificates require. And they feel checking accounts will give them the full service convenience to counter the banker's convenience of "one stop banking."

To commercial bankers the above reasoning seems contradictory. The thrifts appear to desire all the powers the banks have, but at the same time they want the commercials limited in their own ability to compete with the thrifts by the continuation of the Regulation Q interest rate differential and by the continuation of reserve requirements and other restraints that the thrifts do not wish to accept along with the broadened powers.

On the asset side, the thrifts want diversification as well. They recognize by now that their future depends upon earning power. It is not enough to have the power to pay higher rates than the banks can pay; they want additional power to earn these rates. Thus the thrifts want flexible powers to enable them to offer installment loans, variable rate mortgages—whose yields rise as general interest rates rise—and other more profitable lending services.

In sum, they want to become full-service financial institutions for the individual, and they are fighting to obtain these powers with all the political muscle and mental agility they have.

Yet as the thrifts fight the commercial banks, they look over their shoulders and see the rapid development of the credit union as a competitor to both themselves and the banks.

Just as the savings banks and savings and loans were the "fair haired boys" in the 1940s and 1950s—given tax preferences and regulatory benefits that the banks did not have—they themselves are now subject to higher and higher taxes and more and more regulatory intervention. And they see the credit unions behind them, taking advantage of their "common bond" to attract depositors and borrowers, their tax-free status, and their growing powers to accept deposits and make mortgages and other loans. To top this, they see many credit unions happily offering their members the share draft—or a checking account that offers interest and which allows the individual to keep earning interest even after he has written his draft until that draft clears the distant bank on which it was written and the credit union is finally notified to take the money out of the draft writer's account. No wonder so many thrift executives feel that their motto must be "diversify or die."

Men Not Laws

The interesting aspect of the thrift industry dilemma for the student of economics and political science is how much the thrifts have been able to accomplish in their fight for diversification without gaining any new legislative benefits from Congress. Through ingenious use of present legislative powers, the thrifts have been able to accomplish much of what they want in the way of diversification. Consider the following examples.

The NOW account. Faced with the necessity of gaining checking account authority, the thrifts had approached the Congress and the state legislatures for this broadened power but to no avail. Yet, in one instance in Massachusetts, an ingenious thrift executive, Ron Haselton, President of the Consumer's Savings Bank of Worcester, Massachusetts, found a hole in the law through which he drove the proverbial ten-ton truck.

Learning that the state would not allow his savings bank to offer checking accounts, Haselton convinced the State Supreme Court in 1972 that there was no legal prohibition against so-called "negotiable orders of withdrawal"—under which an individual keeps his money in an interest-earning savings account but can remove it by writing a negotiable order of withdrawal against it when he needs money.

To bankers this was nothing but a check. But law can be a funny animal, and the Massachusetts State Supreme Court did see a difference between NOWs and checks. Thus the whole development of interest on checking accounts was inaugurated, which has already spread to all New England and is likely to become nationwide in the next few years.

It was as simple as that—one man's perseverance and ingenuity breaking down a prohibition against checking accounts at thrifts that had been in effect since their start.

Hinky Dinky and the POS terminal. In a similar vein, in Lincoln, Nebraska, John Dean, the guiding light of First Federal Savings and Loan Association of Lincoln, felt that he must find a way to induce the public to take money out of high-cost time certificates and place it back into regular savings accounts, with their lower interest rate payments.

Seeing that some new incentive was needed to achieve this switch back to regular savings, Dean developed a program under which people could move money into and out of their savings accounts not only in the lobby of the savings and loan but also in the Hinky Dinky Supermarket's various locations.

The procedure was simple. Funds were moved through the use of a simple inexpensive plastic card-reading terminal that had been utilized in the thrift institution's lobby. All that had to be done was to place a similar terminal in the supermarket and connect it to the thrift's computer by phone lines. Yet the Hinky Dinky experiment changed the thrift industry. Now the public could have its money earning interest in a thrift institution and at the same time have the convenience of making deposits and withdrawals when shopping at Hinky Dinky. It was as good as interest on checking and in some instances better. But basically, utilizing the point of sale (POS) terminal idea that John Dean had developed, no thrift institution ever again would be limited to accepting deposits and making withdrawal payments only in its own lobby.

And although some states still consider a POS terminal to be a branch, and limit its introduction, as we shall see in the next chapter, even this barrier is breaking down because of the popular public acceptance of this idea.

Telephonic transfer of funds. In addition to the POS terminal, the thrifts are developing other means of offering checking account service on interest-bearing savings accounts, notable among which is the telephonic transfer of funds. The saver earns money on his account until he wants to use it to pay bills. And only then does he call the thrift and have the money transferred to the institution to which he owes the money.

Broader asset powers. Finally, the thrifts are broadening their asset powers. And again this is being done both through broader legislative approval and through innovative usage of traditional powers.

The consumer loan—as a means of generating higher income on a shorter-term asset—is being developed in those states where this is legal for thrifts. And the variable-rate mortgage is being offered as a means of gaining for the thrift the greater flexibility in mortgage lending that fixed-rate mortgages do not provide.

Naturally many individuals do not like the variable-rate mortgage. They much prefer the old approach under which the customer obtains a mortgage which he can keep at predetermined fixed rates if interest rates then rise but which he can refinance if interest rates later fall. Everyone likes a game of "heads I win, tails I don't play."

But the thrifts are making these variable-rate mortgages more attractive by offering incentives such as a lower initial rate and easy prepayment terms. More important, in the states and institutions where the variable-rate mortgage is legal, many thrifts have decided that all loans over a certain size must be through such mortgages. And this is the ultimate inducement to a potential home buyer who wants a large loan, in effect forcing him to accept the newer concept of a variable rate, with his interest payments tied to money market interest rate levels.

In time, moreover, many thrifts feel that they will solve the borrowing-short, lending-long problem and the borrowing-long, lending-short problem as well, by offering both flexible-mortgage rates and flexible-interest rates on savings. This will mean that the spread between cost of funds and returns on funds that the savings banks and savings and loans will earn will remain fairly fixed over time. And the efficiency of operating within that spread rather than the vagaries of the money market will determine the profitability of the savings institution. Thus over time one can see the thrifts winning or gaining every power that the commercial banks have to serve the individual.

And although the thrifts say today that they do not want the power to service business firms as well, many skeptical commercial bankers feel that once the thrifts have the power to serve the individual in all his needs, they will then push for even broader powers.

Many bankers believe that in time, unless the banks fight back, the thrifts will have all the powers the banks have but with far fewer restraints. It is against this possibility that the bankers are beginning their counterattack and responsive plans.

The Banker's Response

One basic result of the growing demand for powers from the thrifts has been that commercial bankers have finally developed a greater political aggressiveness than they utilized in the past. Only when, in early 1976, the thrifts went to Washington and almost succeeded in obtaining legislation to give them most of the banker's powers without any of the restraints and with the continuation of the Regulation Q differential, did the bankers wake up to the fact that they too must tell their story to legislators if they are to remain viable institutions. Moreover the commercial banks have done a good job in telling this story.

Furthermore, many bankers have accepted the "if you can't lick them, join them" approach on the point-of-sale terminals, telephonic transfer of funds, and NOW account service—where such devices are legal for banks.

Even though these ideas were basically developed by the thrifts, the banks were quick to see their popularity among the customers of financial services. Now the banking industry has not only imitated the thrifts, but in many areas it has taken the lead, once the thrifts had introduced these new means of offering convenience and yield to the nation's savers.

Many thoughtful bankers have also analyzed what is happening and have decided that the wholesale invasion of the thrifts into provinces that used to belong exclusively to the bankers requires a reevaluation of the type of accounts that bankers want and the selectivity that they will use in soliciting the public's business.

Most bankers well recognize that the one thing they cannot fight is the competition giving away the business. The thrifts are starting from a base of zero in building checking account balances, whereas the banks find that every time they offer interest on checking they are starting to pay for money they formerly obtained without interest cost. This is why the thrifts can afford to be more aggressive in competing to induce the public to bring its money into interest-bearing checking accounts or at least into savings accounts that offer the convenience of money transfer service.

Thus the bankers are becoming more selective, and they are beginning to compete only for the more profitable business, while letting the thrifts solicit a general gamut of customers whose accounts range from the profitable to the unprofitable. In New England, where both banks and thrifts can offer interest-bearing NOW accounts, the banks have been far less aggressive in providing free NOW accounts—free of service charges and with no minimum balance requirements—than have the thrifts. As a result, the banks have been getting the larger sized balances while the thrifts have been getting more of the average sized deposits, with their higher costs and lower potential for profit.

Yet as both banks and thrifts examine the profitability and costs of NOW accounts, both appear to be retreating from free NOWs by assessing service charges and imposing minimum balance requirements to help make the accounts more profitable.

Another point the commercial bankers are learning is that the thrifts cannot be prevented from offering *some* kind of funds-transfer service. As indicated above, the thrifts feel that obtaining funds-transfer powers of some kind is absolutely vital for their survival. And although they prefer non-interest-bearing demand deposits and non-interest-bearing NOW accounts (NINOWs) to interest-bearing NOW accounts, because the former are obviously cheaper to handle, they will fight like tigers to obtain some form of checking account powers, be it with or without interest. They well recognize that to survive in today's financial environment without strong funds-transfer powers is well-nigh impossible.

Bank Pricing

Ultimately, the development of new services of thrifts and the growth of interest on checking may well be blessings in disguise for the commercial banking industry. Banks are being forced to reevaluate their entire pricing schedule and make banking more efficient.

Few, if any, bankers feel that interest on checking will be a boon to the consumer in the United States. As matters now stand, the banks' inability to offer interest on checking accounts means that banks, by not paying interest on such accounts, penalize large depositors. But conversely, the smaller depositor has an account whose cost to the bank is far greater than is the income the bank receives from it. In fact, because checking accounts are so cheap, the public has a tendency to use checks far more than is necessary. As a result, large depositors are subsidizing the small depositors because of the way service charges are assessed.

But if banks start paying interest on checking accounts, they will have to charge the public more for checking and other services to compensate for this higher cost of demand deposit balances. And this means that the small account, which up to now has been so cheap for the public to maintain, will become more and more expensive. If the public is forced to pay the actual cost of checking service (some banks estimate that it costs up to 52 cents to handle one check), then many people may find that checking accounts as we know them today are beyond their financial reach.

But this too has its bright side. Presumably, if the public is forced to pay the actual cost of checking account service, it will become willing to help the banks reduce the costs of handling funds transfer, provided the public benefits through lower prices.

And in the same way that the telephone company has switched much traffic from operator-handled calls to automatic calling by offering substantial rate reductions for non-operator-handled calls, the banking industry is likely to offer reduced service charges (or no service charges at all) for transactions that are automatically initiated through point-of-sale terminals, through telephonic transfer of funds, and through other methods that re- duce or eliminate the expensive paper trail and reduce the use of personnel.

To bankers this is the bright side of the coin. The other side is that the thrift institutions of the United States—savings banks, savings and loans, and credit unions alike—will never again be satisfied to remain specialized financial services, each one filling a small niche in the overall financial picture. Rather each will adopt the attitude "what's mine is mine and what's yours is nego- tiable." As a result, banking will face more and more competition from the thrift industry in every sphere of commercial banking operations.

One might conclude that in time the thrifts may become so similar to commercial banks that the differences among the vari- ous types of institutions we know today will disappear. But whether we see this actual blending or whether we see separate institutions with similar functions, the commercial bankers know that their days of exclusive control over many segments of the financial marketplace are over.

Acute bankers now accept this trend, and have resolved that their solution is not to oppose changes but to make sure that as the thrifts gain more powers, they also inherit the requirements and responsibilities that bankers must bear. Far more important, they also recognize that even though the competition is becoming more and more aggressive, bankers can prevail. By careful pric- ing, marketing, and evaluating just what type of business they do want and what they can give away, the commercial bankers can meet these new competitive threats and can still be the masters of their own viability and profitability.

11

The Banking Structure in Flux

Although banking as an industry can face the growing competition of thrift institutions and still remain profitable and viable, the changes that thrift competition and new electronic banking techniques are imposing on the industry are still likely to bring marked changes in the structure of banking. These in turn may bring basic changes in how American banking is organized and even as to which banks survive.

When discussing American banking structure, it must be recognized at the outset that our banking system, like the United States government, was planned to provide a minimum of concentration. While England and Canada each have only a handful of banking organizations, the United States has over 14,400. Similarly, to avoid centralization of control, the United States has broken up its central banking structure into twelve Federal Reserve district banks, instead of having one central bank, as do other nations. It was this same desire to avoid centralization that led the United States to establish a federal structure with the functions of government divided between the federal government and the various states.

Banking is also broken up into state-chartered and federally-chartered banks, so that the individual bank is not completely dependent upon one set of charterers and regulators; rather it has the alternative of switching from federal to state charter and regulation or vice versa if the actions of the bank's regulators prove too onerous.

Still, the American banking system of today represents a compromise between two differing philosophies of what a banking system's function should be, because it is subject to considerable control from the Federal Reserve—so that monetary management can be effective—and yet is composed of many units—to promote competition and to give the individual banks as much freedom as possible from central control and establishment of uniform banking policy.

Unit Versus Branch Banking

In the United States, the most significant factors in bank structure are that there is virtually no interstate banking and there are major differences between states in the regulations about the number of offices a bank is allowed to have.

At this writing, in about half the states banks may have branch offices throughout the state to collect deposits, make loans, and carry out the policies established by the headquarters of the bank; in about a third of the states branching is limited, the bank being allowed to establish branches in its own county only or in a limited district within a certain radius of its home office; in the rest of the states no branches at all are allowed, and a bank's operations must be complete within one building.[1] Absolute proscription of branch offices leads to what is called *unit banking,* and this is the only type of bank operation allowed in fewer than a dozen states.

Hybrids have developed, owing to the differences in state laws. In some unit-banking states, bank holding companies have been established. Corporations own a controlling interest in a number of individual banks, and thus provide centralized ownership of a number of banking offices while each bank remains an individual operation, according to unit banking laws. In the unit-banking states where holding companies operate, the law merely restricts the combination of more than one banking office into a single bank; it does not prohibit common ownership of two or more banks by the same corporation, as long as the federal requirements have been met regarding the incorporation of a bank into a holding company.

Holding companies also operate in limited branching states, combining into a statewide or regional network the ownership of unit and branch banks that could not otherwise so combine. Even in states where statewide branching is allowed, holding companies operate, their main goal generally being the placement under

[1]Sometimes a few limited-service accommodation offices nearby are also allowed.

common ownership of banks that operate in different states. (With a few minor exceptions, this is the only way in which interstate bank operations have developed in the United States. The exceptions are offices established in major cities, such as New York, that can be utilized only for international banking operations and not for the transaction of strictly domestic banking business, and branch offices established over state lines before the laws preventing this were passed—in one case, before the territory where the branches were established became a state of the United States.)

In addition to unit banking, branch banking, and holding companies (often called group banking), there is one further way in which banks combine. This is through what is called chain banking, or ownership of the controlling interest in a number of banks by one person or one group of people though not through a corporate structure, unlike holding companies. This informal centralization of control generally occurs in those states where holding companies are not legal or in those instances where the buyers of the bank stock feel that a request for the establishment of a formal holding company would be turned down by the regulatory authorities.

From the viewpoint of the commercial banks' role of middlemen in the process of transmission of credit control's impact to the economy, the vast number of small units in the banking network can serve as a decided handicap to effective implementation of monetary policy decisions, a handicap moderated, however, by the fact that the bulk of bank assets are in the hands of the larger banks.[2]

Whereas unit banking laws are intended to protect the states that use them from the monopoly power of concentrated banking operations, in effect, in many instances they have led to local monopolies in one-bank towns, which face no competition and thus become rather unaggressive in their operations.

Many unit banks, therefore, are poor transmitters of credit control's impact, because they are motivated neither to increase lending in periods of credit ease nor to allocate funds in periods of tight money. Since many of them have monopoly power in their communities and do not face competition from other institutions, they

---

[2]For example, banks of $100 million or more in deposits account for only about 7 percent of all commercial banks, but they hold far more than two-thirds of all commercial bank assets.

see much less of the pressure on profits that forces the shifts in policy over the business cycle, as do banks with more competition.

Furthermore, many of the unit banks in the nation are so small that it is not worthwhile for them to adjust to changes in monetary policy. If the excess reserves a bank generates in a period of credit ease are minor in size, the added profitability derived from changing the bank's aggressiveness in lending and investing is also minor. Thus many small unit banks continue with a fairly stable posture—in tight money times as well as in easy money periods—interest rates charged on loans remaining static and no effort being made to increase or decrease the number of borrowing customers over the credit cycle.

Evidence of this is available from the fact that even in periods of extremely tight credit in the nation—times at which the banking system has faced such a credit squeeze that banks overall were in debt to the Federal Reserve for over $3 billion for loans through the discount window—still there were over $100 million of excess reserves sitting idle in the hands of small member banks throughout the nation, plus the excess funds of nonmember banks, which are generally the smallest banks in the country and thus least able to use excess reserves effectively.[3]

[3]The non-member-bank problem is a growing issue. At present only 5,700 of the nation's 14,400 banks are members of the Federal Reserve System. And while the nonmembers only hold a quarter of the assets of the banking industry, this percentage is growing steadily as more and more state-chartered banks leave the Fed. (Nationally chartered banks must remain as members.) The banks leave because the Fed pays no interest on reserves, while many states allow nonmembers to keep reserves in earning assets such as Treasury bills. And even when the law of the state requires that reserves must be kept in demand deposit form in correspondent banks, the correspondents generally provide a large number of services to entice nonmember reserves, services that are worth a great deal in dollars and cents.

Again this does not lessen the effectiveness of credit control measures. The Fed still determines the total quantity of money in the economy. But, as with near money held in savings institutions, it does cause inequity. The member banks must bear the brunt of the burden of the Fed's reserve requirements, while the banks that are nonmembers do not share in the cost of idling funds at Federal to make credit control work.

The inequity involved may eventually be evened out through allowing the Fed to pay interest on reserves, through member banks' being allowed to keep some of their reserves in earning assets themselves, or through the Fed charging for check clearance and other services now provided free to all banks and giving an offsetting earnings credit to members for deposits held at Federal. If the trend to nonmembership goes too far, we may eventually see Congress requiring all banks that want Federal Deposit Insurance (which is virtually the entire industry) also to be members of the Fed.

The result could be similar to that of pulling on a rope with considerable slack in it; instead of having a taut credit line between the Federal Reserve and the economy, there is this $100 million of slack plus the slack of the nonmember banks. All this money generally has remained as slack, but it could be potentially utilized by these small banks, either directly, through lending and investment activity, or indirectly (by member banks only), through the loan of excess reserves to other banks in need of reserves (through the process called *selling federal funds*, lending reserves held at Federal by one bank to another).

In addition to the uncertainty over the impact of credit control that could develop when monetary policy must be exercised through many small banks, the regional impact of credit control is muddied by the large number of banks and strict geographical limitations on banking in the nation. Credit control is a broad-based indirect control over the quantity of reserves in the banking system rather than a precise attack on certain spending areas or geographical regions.

It may well be that one region of the nation needs credit at a time when another has excess funds available. What is needed at such a time is a banking system able to channel funds from the regions of credit excess to those in need of funds, and here a nationwide bank could quickly adjust its lending policy to even out the disparity. However, with over 14,400 separate banks, the process of channeling funds to where they are needed is usually good but sometimes a little slow and inexact, and the impact of credit restraint or ease can be somewhat less smooth than the nation's economy needs.

To summarize, credit control is only as effective as the aggressiveness and imagination of the banks that serve as its transmitters allow it to be. In a nation with a large number of small banking units, many of which are not motivated by profit considerations or which hesitate to change policies for reasons of inertia, the impact of credit control is perforce blunted to a degree.

The Trend to Merger

One point must be stressed. There is no automatic correlation between size of bank unit and aggressiveness. Many of the most aggressive banks in the nation are small unit banks, and as such these are excellent transmitters of the Federal Reserve's credit policies. Some large branch banking systems are not aggressive, and hinder credit control's effectiveness just as unaggressive small banks do. As a general rule, however, small banks are less aggressive and less viable units than large banks, for the following reasons.

1. Small banks do not have the resources to make it worthwhile to shift policy sharply over the business cycle, because the total impact of such a shift on their dollars-and-cents earnings generally would not be very large.

2. Small banks do not have staffs large enough to allow for talent in depth in both lending and investment. In other words, policies often remain unchanged because there are not enough people on hand who are able to implement shifts to more aggressive lending policy even if the value of these shifts is understood.

3. Small banks cannot afford to train new manpower to the same extent as large banks, cannot afford to provide backup talent to the top men in most areas, and cannot afford to have specialists in such areas as marketing, investment, and trust services.

4. Small banks do not have the resources to meet growing credit demands of their borrowing customers as these customers grow. They are further hampered in this regard by the limit on the percent of capital that can be loaned to a single borrower. Thus many successful customers outgrow their banks, and the bank is left serving the small, less successful business firm in the community while the prospering companies move on to larger banks in nearby larger communities.

5. Small banks generally cannot afford the expensive equipment, such as computers, that is now becoming a necessity for efficient, economical handling of the paper work of banking.

In addition to these deficiencies in small banking units, all of which point to eventual amalgamation into larger banking units, other factors also have led to a merger movement in banking, which is still only in its early stages but which is likely to affect even the states that today allow only unit banking.

1. The shifting of the American population from small communities to cities is lessening the need for financial facilities in small

towns and thus making the small unit bank in these areas less viable.

2. There is a problem of management succession in many small banks, which results from the lack of trained personnel on hand. When the top officer of the bank dies or retires, there is often no manager available to take over.

3. Because many small banks find that their stock is much harder to sell than that of larger banks which have more shares outstanding, there is a problem of divesting stock ownership without serious sacrifice of value when the owners of a small bank die or want to sell out. By merging their bank into a larger institution, however, the owners are often able to avoid this future problem by turning in their shares for the more widely held and traded shares of the larger bank.

4. The developing trend of remote banking is lessening the customer's dependence upon the convenience of the banking office.

Already Americans cash more checks in supermarkets than they do in banks. Their payroll checks are being deposited automatically, and now the credit card is reducing the need to visit the bank for a loan. With a bank credit card, the customer is given a maximum line of credit that he can use, and then, as long as he makes periodic payments to keep his outstanding loan below the maximum, he can borrow again and again by paying for goods and services with his credit card instead of coming into the bank to negotiate a personal loan for each item he wants to buy.

With efforts now being made to have routine bills paid automatically and to have funds moved from a purchaser's bank account into that of the vendor through credit card activation of point-of-sale terminals that are connected by direct wire with the banking industry's computers, individuals find less and less need to visit their bank's office.

The result is that unit banks now are beginning to face competition from other institutions in nearby and even quite distant towns, and the local monopoly status of some banks is being broken by these changes in technology. The answer of some small banks has often been to join large banking enterprises so that they can attract customers on a service basis rather than rely mainly on the basis of convenience of location.

Other banks have taken the approach of fighting the encroachment of the remote banking terminals of other institutions by claiming in court that they are actually branches rather than mere point-of-sale terminals or automatic teller machines. And when state law prohibits branching, they have often been able to delay this electronic expansion of potential competitors by winning many of these suits.

Finally others of these smaller independent banks have taken the attitude that they can turn electronic banking to their advantage. If people can bank at remote institutions through automatic deposit of payroll checks, through credit card borrowing, and through use of point-of-sale terminals interconnected throughout the nation, then the local bank can keep the accounts and business of local people who have migrated elsewhere in search of better employment opportunities. Although our nation is becoming more urban and suburban, many smaller rural banks feel they will be able to remain viable by serving remote customers through an environment of electronic banking, just as small independent telephone companies remain viable by hooking into the networks of the Bell System and other majors for provision of long distance service.

5. With banks able to switch between state and national charters, there is a sort of competition between the various regulatory bodies to be generous in approving merger requests where state law allows, lest the banks involved move to the regime of another regulatory agency.

6. This liberalization of banking regulation is being accompanied also by a slow breakdown in the restraints on branch banking in the state legislatures. Part of this breakdown is being caused by a feeling that the economy of the state can be better served by larger banking units; some pressure is even beginning to come from those unit bankers who realize the advantages to themselves of the option of joining larger branch bank or holding company organizations.

In this effort to expand the size of banking and lessen the dependence of American banking on the small bank unit, however, there is opposition from the antitrust officers of the Justice Department and from the Supreme Court. It has been the feeling of the Justice Department, corroborated by the Court in the 1963 case

United States v. Philadelphia National Bank *et al.,* 374 U.S. 321, that banking is a unique line of commerce; each bank competes only with other commercial banks, and when merger of two or more banks into one organization is allowed, it restrains competition in the banking industry.

There is good reason to believe that even this roadblock to larger banking organizations will eventually be demolished. Banks do not compete only with other banks. Rather, in all areas of operations, each bank finds itself competing with the various financial intermediaries, with the money and capital markets, with the ability of corporations to finance themselves through internal generation of cash, and with government financing units.

In fact, it might be said that as competition develops in lending and in attracting deposit funds, each financial institution reacts by taking on more of the services of its competitors in an attempt to avoid the earnings squeeze through diversification. Banks have entered the savings and mortgage markets in competition with savings banks and savings and loan associations; banks are making more term loans, competing with the longer-term lending of insurance companies and pension funds; savings banks and savings and loans are working to enter the installment lending areas, since they face competition in their traditional loan outlet, the mortgage market. The choice of the borrowing customer becomes wider and wider.

Similarly, as we have seen, in deposit solicitation the banks not only have become major competitors with other financial intermediaries and money market instruments for the available funds of the public, but some major banks have also started to move beyond their home markets and solicit funds nationally. This has been done by national marketing of their time certificates of deposit.

An analogy might be made with railroad regulation. When the railroads were first regulated, it was because they had a monopoly on inland transportation, and governmental regulation was necessary to protect the public. Now, however, when the choice available to shippers is so much greater, the railroad monopoly has virtually disappeared, and the trend in railroad regulation is toward less, rather than more, government control over rates charged and services offered.

Similarly, the banks are now facing competition from other

financial institutions in every area. The entire financial community is engaged in a trend toward what might be called *scrambled finance,* each type of institution becoming more like its competitors, and each bank and financial intermediary competing more with other institutions in its own industry as well as with institutions in other phases of the financial structure.

Banking is changing as the nation changes. In time these changes will be reflected in a relaxation of the restraints on the formation of larger banking units. In addition, the regulatory policy in other areas, including credit control, will have to change to match the changes in the institutional structure of banking and thrift institution operations, so that the impact of credit control will be more evenly distributed over the entire financial community.

As for the structure of banking, it is obvious that our nation does not need all the banks and thrift institutions in existence today. With remote banking techniques developing, we will have less and less reason to visit a bank or savings institution. Banking then will become like a public utility. All of us use electricity and telephones. Yet few of us have ever had a need to visit the powerhouse or the telephone exchange. As a result we will choose our bank or thrift on the basis of service quality, attractiveness of interest rates paid, and economy of loan rates charged, rather than because it is closest to home.

As indicated above, the growing mobility of banking service should be no threat to the independent bank or thrift that is doing its job and remains competitive in rates and service. It will be able to keep its home-town customers no matter where they move. For banks and thrifts that are not watching costs and services and which become uncompetitive, however, the advantages of convenience of location will no longer serve to offset these other drawbacks, and these institutions will undoubtedly be forced out of existence.

Commercial banking is thus an industry in flux, and the changes in bank structure will be significant in the years ahead. But changes in structure and competition will not be the only new departures for the industry. In many other areas, ranging from pricing to personnel, banking is likely to be a different industry a decade from now than it is today. It is on these prospective changes that the final chapter of this volume will focus.

12

Where Is Banking Headed?

It is hard to look at the future of banking without first looking backward to see how most forecasts made by banking observers a decade earlier have turned out. Although we thought banking would change dramatically in the 1970s, it has just not turned out that way. The directions predicted have been correct. But the degree of change has been far more modest than predicted.

Some of the predictions included the following.

1. Banks would diversify to such a point that major institutions would no longer be just banks. Rather they would be full financial service vehicles in which banking was only one of the many services offered the public.

2. Liability management would free the major banks from the restraints of credit control policy. The only limit that would be set on their ability to meet loan commitments and fund investment opportunities would be their willingness to pay going rates for money.

3. Scientific management and operations research would enable banks to make decisions based more on fact and less on hunches and opinions. "The computer's great strength is logic and its great weakness is paper handling. Yet the banks use the computer mainly for paper handling." Observers thus felt the computer would enable banking to switch to scientific decision making.

4. The checkless society would be a reality, with automatic funds transfer replacing the check for most routine transactions.

5. Banks would be earning about as much of their income from the sale of services and talent as from lending and investing money.

6. Finally, we would see fewer and larger banks, with the total number shrinking from 13,500 to between 5,000 and 7,000 by the end of the decade.

190

Obviously, banking changes did not come about as predicted.

1. The banking industry learned, after experimenting with running finance companies, operating mortgage companies, establishing real estate investment trusts, and undertaking other measures of diversification, that the traditional banking functions of taking deposits and making loans are pretty good business by themselves. And some of the banks that used their holding companies as vehicles for diversification have now retreated by spinning off the new ventures and going back to basic banking.

2. As Chapter Nine argued, aggressive liability management created more troubles for banking and the economy than it was worth. Banking has thus retreated markedly from the experiments of the late 1960s and of 1973 and 1974, in which aggressive banks tried to buy their way out of the impact of tight money.

3. Despite scientific management and operations research, banking remains a people business; and decisions are still based on experience, hunches, and opinions.

4. The checkless society has come about far less rapidly than predicted and with far more bank customers than expected objecting to the elimination of checks.

5. Banks are still basically selling money, not service and talent.

6. Finally, whereas we had 13,500 banks a decade ago, we now have 14,400, owing to the fact that the chartering of new banks vastly exceeded the number of mergers and acquisitions.

Thus, as we look at the changes expected in the decade ahead, all observers of the banking scene have become more modest in their expectations of new trends and techniques.

Changes Expected

One point can be made with certainty, however. Banking will be far more competitive than in the past. The concept of scrambled finance, under which each type of financial institution is trying to encroach on everyone else's territory, is giving the public far more choices than previously as to where and how to bank. We are seeing savings banks, savings and loan associations, credit unions, and finance companies diversifying into spheres that formerly were served by commercial banks alone. And we are even seeing brokerage firms take the excess funds in a customer's securities account and place them in a vehicle that allows automatic investment in a money market fund and yet allows easy withdrawal through a draft or a debit card. On top of this, the account holder can also overdraw and get cash using the value of his securities held as collateral.

To banks, the result has already been a greater emphasis on return on assets and return on capital, whereas in the past banks were more concerned about comparative size and growth rates. The competitive environment is making profits much harder to come by than in the past.

The regulatory environment of banking should also see marked changes. As we have indicated in earlier chapters, there should be a relaxation of the Regulation Q ceiling for all institutions, and easing of branching and holding company acquisition powers, and an expansion of the number and types of financial institutions subject to the kinds of restraints that have been imposed to make credit control effective.

At the same time, it is likely that we will see more and more intervention by the Federal Reserve and other regulatory and legislative forces into the money and capital markets under the broad concept of credit allocation. Whether for good or evil, the authorities of the nation are far less willing than in the past to allow banks to determine the allocation of credit solely on the basis of balancing risk, income, and liquidity.

As for geographical expansion, we have seen above that the developing utilization of electronic funds transfer is giving banks the ability and opportunity of serving customers located far from where the bank's office happens to be. And through the use of shared POS terminals and telephonic transfer of funds, we will see banking offer the public the convenience of a public utility. But there will be the added competition that will derive from the disappearance of local monopolies. If a bank is not offering top-quality service and competitive rates, people will be able to bank with institutions located elsewhere just as conveniently as they can bank with the hometown people.

But here a warning must be issued. We had thought ten years ago that trends in geographic expansion would lead to the extinction of the community bank, and we were wrong. The local organization is a hardy breed. It can provide most customer services and, knowing its customers intimately, it can make quick decisions on credits. We are likely to see some decline in the number of individual banks and even in the number of banking offices, as automatic terminals provide the convenience the public wants and needs. But the number of banks will decline only slowly; for many Americans like their local community banks and will stick with them unless service and prices become so out of line that they are forced to switch. And this is not likely to happen to too many independent institutions.

Where banks exist simply because the law has not allowed branching, and where all that is needed is a small, lightly staffed branch, the efforts at more efficient banking should lead to merger and acquisition. And in all cases, we are likely to see fewer marble buildings and more modest-sized, movable bank facilities, with storefront branches becoming more popular when terminals cannot do the full job in serving a locality.

The day when America is down to 5,000 or fewer banks, however, still appears far in the future. People like the community bank, and where the banking business is adequate to support an independent organization, we are not likely to see the bank swallowed up by larger institutions, except in those cases where the banker is just not doing the job.

In sum, banking service will cross community, county, and state lines, and in a few instances and under reciprocal agreements between states, bank organizations may even obtain permission to branch in neighboring states. But the unusual combination of large and small banks and thrifts surviving together that has characterized the financial structure of this nation will remain intact.

Bank Service

We know that bankers are retreating from their ventures into broad-scale diversification undertaken in at least the preceding ten years. History shows that in many instances these outside activities caused serious trouble for the bank holding companies that undertook them. First, they involved a type of aggressiveness and risk taking that was not indigenous to banking and bank people. And second, the banks did not have the proper talent to run these organizations. Certainly banking will continue to operate to a degree in these nonbank areas, but the major attention will return to commercial banking.

Even in the securities area, in which we hear frequent stories of possible bank competition against securities firms, there is not likely to be too much bank expansion. Laws and regulations limit bank expansion, and many bankers just do not see profits in these areas of heavy paper work and high risk.

This is not to say that banking is likely to remain static in the providing of services. Rather it appears that instead of continuing to look to distant areas for growth opportunities, banking will try to develop services as offshoots of present banking operations. For example, we are likely to see bankers offering more help to customers in bill paying, inventory control, tax preparation, and the other areas of financial documentation and funds flow that can be tied to the handling of the payments function.

In addition, bankers now know that electronic funds transfer will not become the major force for the less-check society and the reduction of paper handling that bankers hope it will be unless and until the industry is able to offer the public something more than just the elimination of checks (and of the public's cherished float).

These financially related bookkeeping and payments services should become more important, both for individuals and for business firms, as banks try to become full financial counselors on money management and flow rather than merely the movers of money through the nation.

People

Another area of certainty is that banks will require more skilled personnel with more diverse training than in the past. One lesson of the late 1960s and early 1970s is that machines will not replace financial judgment. We had thought that we would see operations research techniques and scientific management help banking do its job and help make more accurate and impersonal decisions about granting credit, pricing services, establishing branches, controlling investments, and the like. What we found was that the machines cannot replace good training and intuition and years of experience.

Yet if banking is to prosper, it must become a more capital-intensive and less labor-intensive industry. And this is happening. We are reducing the number of people needed to handle routine bank functions, and the developments of EFTS should reduce this need even more. Banking also faces a problem in middle management; there simply will not be as much need for middle managers whose function is managing the staffs in entry and lower-level positions. What is needed instead is a type of individual who can help provide the personal financial service to the bank's customers mentioned above.

We are likely, then, to see a change in banking that will markedly alter the traditional career paths. Increasingly, outsiders who have talents needed for the more complex banking services will be hired and fewer opportunities will develop for people to move up from entry-level positions into bank management. The result will be even greater pressure on banking to reduce the number of clerical and routine eimployees, because the aggressive employees, lacking the opportunities they used to have and dissatisfied with their static positions, may begin efforts at union organization.

Banking thus will become more and more like the telephone company, where routine operations handle themselves, and the people on the premises are utilized for the exception transactions. Those who move up will have more exciting challenges, but there is likely to be a wider gap between routine jobs and officer jobs than in the past, with fewer opportunities for movement up through the ranks because of the more complex talents needed in higher banking positions.

Profit

With competition growing in the entire financial sector and with diversified services not the boon to bank income they had been expected to be, bank profits will be under squeeze in the years ahead.

Banks formerly had three good sources of profit.

1. Interest rates were rising and banks could earn more year after year.
2. Banks were becoming more aggressive and were switching from low-yielding loans and investments to higher-yielding ones.
3. The public was not too interest-rate sensitive, and banks could get money fairly cheaply.

Now all three advantages have disappeared. The period of the sharp rises in interest rates is over, banks are about as aggressive as they are allowed to be, and the depositor knows the value of his or her funds and wants adequate reward for their use.

Bankers also realize that it will be hard to widen the spread between costs of funds and returns on funds in the competitive environment we face today. So they are recognizing that profits will come to the more efficient banks.

One result of the profits squeeze is that the industry is becoming more earnings conscious and is less interested in volume of funds as the basic determinant of whether a bank is doing a good job. More and more banks are pricing services so that they offer a profit, and if the customer refuses to pay this price because he can get a lower price across the street, the banker is more likely to help him across the street and into the lobby of the competitor and less likely to reduce his price to loss-leader levels than in the past.

In addition, more and more banks are beginning to turn greater attention to the types of customers who truly are dependent upon the banks and who cannot go elsewhere to get cheaper money when the banks try to charge prices for services and credit that are fully compensatory. This means that bankers are concentrating more on serving the medium-sized company that cannot turn to the money market for funds and are downgrading the courting of the larger corporation that has fund sources elsewhere. It also means that if the thrifts are willing to provide checking account services below bank costs and otherwise undercut bank operations by charging rates below what banks can afford to charge, more bankers are becoming resigned to letting the business go elsewhere rather than accepting a loss simply to have larger numbers of accounts and volumes of funds on the books.

Bankers recognize that they will need capital to back growth.

They also know that with bank stocks frequently in public disfavor, they cannot count on tapping the capital market for new equity without seriously eroding the equity positions of present shareholders when bank shares sell below book value, as frequently is the case.

Leverage has been pushed about as far as it can go in many instances. And banks also realize that too much reliance on leveraged capital positions discourages many potential borrowers from using a bank. The borrowers fear that the undercapitalized bank will not be able to give them the credit accommodation they may need at a later date. Thus many banks have decided that they need capital as a sign of strength and as a means of backing growth, but that the only feasible means of getting new capital will be through retained earnings.

This helps explain why bankers are finally switching their emphasis from footings and growth over to profits and the "bottom line." It is a healthy change, and it makes banking more businesslike than in the past in determining which services to provide, how to price them, and what to do if the competition is giving away the bank.

This emphasis on profit is also eliminating the old image of the bank as a comfortable place to work in which no one ever gets fired. The emphasis on profit has forced bankers to be hard nosed in employment policies as in everything else. This includes eliminating employees if the jobs they do no longer are needed or if they are not able to handle the more complex activities that banking now involves.

The conflict involved is a difficult one. Banking, like other industries, has taken upon itself the obligation of meeting social goals in the community, under the principal of long-range self-interest. The basic attitude of the forward-thinking banker is that if the community deteriorates, the bank's prospects will deteriorate too. Thus bankers have been leaders in urban renewal, rural redevelopment, and other programs of social betterment.

Bankers have also taken upon themselves the obligation of training the disadvantaged in banking operations, and banks are working on meeting the spirit and not just the letter of every affirmative action program.

This brings a decided conflict between the social goals of banking and the profit goals. And the effort to meet both conflicting goals helps explain why bankers have been among the leaders in trying to develop new computerized capital-intensive techniques that can make the industry more efficient and generate more income from the greater use of the talent now on board.

To say that banking will solve all its problems of profits squeezes in the next decade, however, is too optimistic an evaluation of the competitive environment and of the jobs that banking has taken upon itself in the interest of the public good. The golden days when banking profits were assured and all banks had earnings growth year after year are far behind us.

This, then, is the banking industry we are likely to see in the decade ahead. It is an industry whose competitors will be far more diverse than in the past, because of the widened powers of formerly specialized competitors such as credit unions and thrift institutions.

It is an industry in which banking will become more impersonal and automatic to save costs of paper handling. Yet it is still trying to carry water on the other shoulder through management information systems, central files, and other automatic devices that can help maintain a full financial picture of the individual and his desires and needs even as his routine banking becomes more automatic.

It is an industry in which the types of financial services offered will be far greater than in the past, and people will find that their banks will be able to take many routine financial tasks off their hands. But people will also find that they will be paying for these services in hard dollars and cents.

It also appears likely that our fixation with cheap money will end, and that banks will be allowed to pay more for time and savings deposits than in the past. But the price for this greater return to the public will have to be higher charges on borrowing customers. If we are truly a capital-short nation, this is only as it should be; the providers of the capital should be amply rewarded for their thrift while those who wish to use other people's money should pay what the funds are worth.

Finally, banking is an industry that will continue to operate with a crazy patchwork structure; banks will range in size from giant multinational organizations with thousands of branches and remote terminals in thousands of other locations, down to the unit bank that may or may not decide to connect to the electronic devices for remote deposit and withdrawal of funds that will be made available to it on a shared cost-and-usage basis.

Yet this is the strength of American banking—the choice offered the public between types of banks and other financial servicers keeps each institution on its toes and leads to innovations such as the NOW account and the point-of-sale terminal as a means of gaining an edge, albeit a temporary one, on one's competitors.

The only development that could truly harm the banking industry would be if its leaders were to become so set against change that they asked the legislators to pass laws prohibiting the type of dynamic change that we have seen. And even then, it is likely that some innovators, either inside the establishment or outside, would find ways around the new laws, just as thrifts got around controls on demand deposits through telephonic transfer of savings funds and the use of point-of-sale terminals and as the public got around interest rate ceilings through disintermediation.

To those who fear change, it should be heartening to remember that the changes ahead will be about as moderate in their development as have been the changes in the recent past, and that the worst fears of what change would do to traditional banking have just not materialized.

But, although banking activities will change and the institutions and bankers that oppose change will undoubtedly end up the worse under the new policies, the key issue remains the position that banks will play in the economy.

This volume has argued that the banks have played a valuable role as the middlemen between the Fed and the economy—transmitting the impact of both tight and easy money from the central bank to the various users of credit in the nation, with the financial principles of risk, income, and liquidity serving as the basic guideposts in this process.

Now, however, considerable pressure is being exerted for greater governmental intervention in this process.

First, as we have seen, there is the desire of some officials for credit allocation. Their expectation is that this will help alter bank lending and investing policy to help achieve social goals to a greater extent, rather than have financial objectives serve as the main determinant of which sectors obtain funds. And as we have also discussed, credit allocation could well lead to a switch from financial to political tenets serving as the prime motivators of bank lending and investing policy, a development that bankers and many other observers strongly fear.

Second, we have seen that Federal Reserve policy has not always been as effective as it could be. And while in theory we can have either inflation or unemployment at any moment of time, in practice we have experienced *stagflation*—or inflation and unemployment simultaneously. Many feel that greater use of an *incomes policy,* involving governmental intervention in the wage- and price-setting mechanism and in the flow of credit, will be necessary to eliminate this apparent paradox. This would also have adverse implications for our present delivery system of credit restraint and ease and for the free functioning of our entire financial community.

Finally, we see efforts such as the growth of government guarantee programs and pressure for strong implementation of usury ceilings that are attempts to give certain sectors preference over other sectors in the attraction of available money and capital market funds. The goal is also to give the favored sectors attractive concessions to make their cost of money lower than normal market conditions would dictate. These efforts at special preference also have adverse implications for the functioning of our free banking system.

We can thus conclude that the basic threat to banking comes from outside the industry—primarily from the regulatory sphere. Banking and the other financial institutions can handle the intense competition that interindustry diversification and expansion efforts have caused. And while some banks and thrifts will fall by the wayside, those which have effective and sensitive managements will adjust to whatever comes along on the competitive scene.

Rather it is the attempts at obtaining regulation and legislation to use our financial mechanism for other, nonfinancial goals that remains the most serious threat to the industry. And the way we compromise our desire to attain social goals through the allocation of funds with our opposing desire to let basic financial principles continue to dictate the allocation of credit in the nation will be the key determinant of what our banking industry and our financial environment look like in the decades hence.

Recommended Reading

Baughn, William H., and Charles E. Walker, eds. *The Bankers Handbook.* Homewood, Ill.: Dow Jones-Irwin, 1978.

Crosse, Howard D., and George H. Hempel. *Management Policies for Commercial Banks.* Englewood Cliffs, N.J.: Prentice-Hall, 1973.

Gies, Thomas G., and Vincent P. Apilado, eds. *Banking Markets and Financial Institutions.* Homewood, Ill.: Irwin, 1971.

Gup, Benton E. *Financial Intermediaries.* Boston: Houghton Mifflin, 1976.

Hailey, Arthur. *The Money Changers.* New York: Doubleday, 1975.

Jacobs, Donald P., Loving C. Farwell, and Edwin Neave. *Financial Institutions.* Homewood, Ill.: Irwin, 1972.

Lindow, Wesley. *Inside the Money Market.* New York: Random House, 1972.

Reed, Edward W., Richard V. Cotter, Edward K. Gill, and Richard K. Smith. *Commercial Banking.* Englewood Cliffs, N.J.: Prentice-Hall, 1976.

Ritter, Lawrence S., and William L. Silber. *Principles of Money Banking and Financial Markets.* New York: Basic Books, 1974.

Woodworth, G. Walter. *The Money Market and Monetary Management.* New York: Harper & Row, 1972.

Index

WITHDRAWN

ABOUT THE AUTHOR

Paul S. Nadler is Professor of Business Administration at Rutgers, The State University of New Jersey. He is also Contributing Editor both of *The American Banker,* the daily banking newspaper, and of *Bankers Monthly* Magazine. He is a consultant on banking and economics to several banks, is consulting economist to L. F. Rothschild, Unterberg, Towbin, and to Louis Harris and Associates, Inc., and for two decades has served as Academic Director of the I.B.M. Graduate School of Banking. He lectures regularly at the Stonier Graduate School of Banking and at the AT&T Advanced School in Finance and originates a monthly tape series, The Bankers Executive Seminar Series. Dr. Nadler is also author of *Paul Nadler Writes About Banking*.